To the ancestors who hold the line,

the grandfather, the grandmother.

To the line of great masters of

mystical imagination,

to the spiral wall of living flame

that guides and loves us all.

To the stillness from which

we all come, and

return.

To the Great spirit, I

humbly give thanks for the awareness

of the present.

Aho Mitakuye Oyasin.

SUN KING

"The majesty of this Neter sails on and arrives at the eleventh door: the one who rebuffs the allies of Seth and at the twelfth hour: the one who sees the beauty of Ra…"

(The Book of Horus)

Sun King

Cover & Artwork by: Front- Marco Camargo, Back-Ryan McMahon

Editing by: Linda Beaulieu

Formatting by: Linda Beaulieu

Contact: sunkingram@gmail.com

Table of Contents

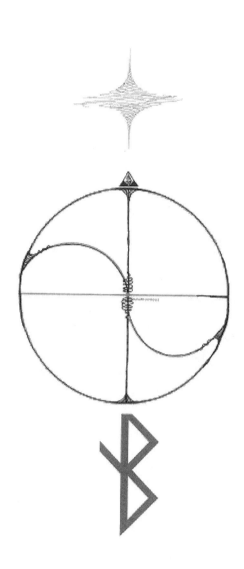

Prologue

If the shining golden orb has a name in any culture he is the Sun. The Most High God is always named the Sun regardless what language the name is spoken in. He is the power source of mankind, and the beautiful Earth we spring from. When speaking of his Creator and Sustainer, it is God or Goddess of no name. It is the force that is causal still magnetic light. The Shining rays of the Sun, the wisest men, do not worship him, as the cause for they know that he is not quite the first cause. And the wisest man's worship can reveal the cause of all things, the creator itself and Sustainer of all forms in the universe. She the creator goddess is causal still magnetic light, and so it is wise for men not to worship the forms or manifestations that she so creates in the electric male energy known as the Sun.

Man should not bend his knee to the forms even with all their beauty and radiance for they are still temporal. The only thing in the universe that truly exists and is not temporal, is the cause, the still magnetic light which is pure potential, and all forms spring from the stillness and all forms dissolve back into it. When we as individual spirits or souls, embark from the cause, the stillness, we are activating a deep seated memory of our divine origins. However, we tend to lose and forget ourselves through amnesia. We forget who and what we really are. The Great Spirit, the cause is still within us always. We descend through the ten rings or Sephiroth or planets or chakras. These rings, these systems create more and more density and more and more dimensions until we finally land here on Earth in the third dimension as material/physical bodies. Simply because we are crystallized into material bodies, we identify our consciousness with matter. This is a mistake, as we should always remember our divine origin as cause, still causal light.

When we descend these rings, we become aware of all forms and manifestation being born of electric light. But male electric light is temporal and spatial, and not eternal. All electric manifestation expresses itself as oneness divided into two sexes or genders. The gender generates more and more manifestation and beauty. These manifestations, these rings, are likened to the greatest macrocosm as well as to the tiniest microcosm. The Sun moves in an elliptic, as well as many other celestial bodies. This ecliptic is the waveform undulation of cyclical infinity. The ancients called it the lamnescate, the infinity symbol. The Sun moves in the ecliptic. Particles, atoms, electrons, protons, and other imaginaries all have their own ecliptic that they are moving around in cycles, and that they also have moving around them in expanding or contracting cycles. This is exactly why all manifestation keeps moving into infinity. This is also why beneath all manifestation is the cause sustaining it.

Self, presents as some sort of reservoir. It knows, but what is knowing or knowledge or what is the difference between the two? I have to say that knowing is better represented by feeling than by thinking or thought. Now I have to think my way through this but when I know something, there is some sort of energetic impulse that is felt in my being through and through. This shows that it's not something that is thought it is something that is felt. And it must be the self, a reservoir that holds and recognizes this feeling. Now we go further into this dynamic, where is the mind located? It's not in the brain. If we were to try to locate it we would have to say it is sensed by the entire body or being and this marks the point that mind is actually the interface between the body and higher consciousness but I guess we can say the spiritual self which is really the self that knows.

The self knows its own center or origin in the universe. Now we get lost often by falling away from the center. Most often it is our society and culture that causes us to lose the feeling of center. We could call this the construct, some people call it the matrix but what it really is is a collective agreed upon version of reality. And it is not a true reality, because it is fueled by every person's fears, anxieties, misconceptions, and confusions as well as fueled with all of our positive traits as well. It's a bit like the self is submerged in some large stew, an agreed upon description of reality. So it's each individual's divine right, and I would say duty to use the imagination and creativity that the self is involved with. This creative awareness, gives each individual self the opportunity to create the dream. And here is a key point here, our construct or society has told us that our sleep and our waking life are different and that our sleep is of no importance, it's just a useless fantasy or a myth. But I have to say this is totally incorrect. Just as the soul/self is moulded and created by our unique perception of reality in waking life, so the soul/self develops a refinement in sleeping consciousness. The self, being aware can potentially gain consciousness in the dreaming state, then shifting perception permanently when reflected upon in waking life. Our prisons can be opened when consciousness glimpses higher worlds, where awareness of its true design and nature resides. Unfoldment is much more fluid than ordinary people perceive.

Once the self becomes centered, it remembers and realizes its divine place in the cosmos, and it realizes that consciousness is not asleep. What this means is that the dream world is just as valid and real as what we would call the waking world. If it were not fundamental, then why do we all do it? We all breathe, we all dream. When the self realizes this, its relationship to itself (the subject-object relationship) nucleates or dissolves or balances. This awareness of balance is transcendence. If you want to use scientific terms, we nucleate our own opposites because we are our own observer. J. Krishnamurti said it like this, the observer and the observed are the same thing, they are one. When the self realizes this, reality occurs. We nucleate our own opposites and the construct dissolves away or falls apart.

Knowing and knowledge are a bit different. Knowledge is an objective accumulation or residue of a thing but not the thing itself. And so knowing, is not information about a thing, it is a feeling or resonance of the thing itself. The knowing arises by intimate energetic exchange with the thing. In this case, the self realizes its own divinity and divine nature...so once the center self realizes its own divine nature and power, if it falls away from the center it is due to some consent. People consent to their own enslavement, because they are afraid to be responsible for themselves and to create their own reality which is our divine right and duty. Sovereignty is the actual design and makeup of the self (reservoir)...it is untouched by others, there's nothing that another person can do to destroy one's self, however, people will tell you otherwise, and when they do, they are asking you to consent to your own destruction. The enslavers simply want to control your consciousness for their own personal use. But of course the self is sovereign and it is everyone's duty to their highest knowing of self, the most authentic self, to transcend the construct which is the programming that society and culture has given to you. Consider your own true divine right to outshine the construct, the current paradigm. Feel that expanse and think freely.

"Several Ways to Here"

Hand-in-hand we face the end. In the tender spaces we begin again. Eyes to see, the brilliant unfolding crime. Shaking when I landed here, I'm told to forget. Feeling empathic waves, the wind and the wet. I am told to forget. Now I'm walking and handed the cross, but only one pocket so it has been lost. Story I am told intrinsic yet forgotten. Our star still shines while the Apple is rotten. The first people's beauty handed to us in Sweet Grass. The heart given to earth…How can you return to the lies of your crooked smiles? Don't you know the river eternal goes on forever?

Hmm, I think I'm awake, awake and must be asleep still. Hard to know at this time. Yes I'm aware of my thoughts, my internal thoughts, I must be awake…I am ever awakening.

We are sensitive energetic beings. We are thought beings by design. Humans can manifest their reality. This is our divine right, which gives rise to our divine will.

Energetic shifts are the works of the true medicine person. See the healing emotional space to be in. Thus the body/mind heals.

Universe = life

World = mind

Time = soul

1
Sleeping Cave

Awake! I feel the stirring of pins and needles tingling in my shins, calf, and legs. I know this as the return from a winter's hibernation. I roll over but only in my mind, my body is still and stiff. I will move and gather my mind about myself and begin to explore what's beyond. I know not what lies out there beyond my cocoon, my cave, the place I've been asleep for what must be an eternity. Time is so cloudy/blurry. Is it yesterday today? I need more time to pick up my inner voice and push it into some direction, some action, but it will be a little while before I muster the energy to open my eyes and greet what's on the other side of these eyelids. I can't even remember how to assemble a world, the world. I must agree with the universe, the great expanse on how to put the vision of the world into coherence.

I'm on the ground and it's comfortable, I pull myself from the earth and unstick my shoulders and back from the membrane of the earth mother. I begin to sit, to make myself up-right. I can feel the blood begin to take form. An energetic bubble of sensory perception is forming. I vaguely remember this feeling from an earlier lifetime, and previous moment. Eyes open, it's still dark. I can only see my thoughts on the inside of my mind, the living mind. It's dark but it's no bother, I am use to it. I am the bear of a deep slumber. Darkness is comforting to me. My inner thoughts are just flashes of light within the darkness and make only fragmentary sense of who/what/where I am.

A hunger begins, first behind my eyes and then in my gut. Food of some sort, some sustenance I am compelled to find. I roll around arms in front of me feeling for boundaries, a guide post, and a direction. After some time floundering like this I drop my arms and begin to feel with a pulse of energy emanating from my navel. From here I detect a balance as I walk in the darkness. My navel leads and I can sense a roof and walls around me. I labor on until a ray of light kisses my right cheek, I know where to go. I inhale the ray of light, and it grows to wash me in full light of a solar nature. I am at the opening of a cave. My eyes adjust, taking in colors, lights, swirls, geometric shapes, and stars. It comes into an image, a focus of a vista. I peer through a window into a brand new reality, one I've never seen before although it's made of familiar forms and smells.

A bending ravine type path, I follow down and out of the cave. It's no longer dark. I see trees, and leaves rustling coupled with blue skies and round clouds. It's cool and a shiver whips my neck and ears. I didn't know it was warm and comfortable in the cave until the contrast of this ravine trail. I stretch my chest, arms, and legs into this new birth. I am food bound and seeking. I am exploring the unknown territory with which my eyes and senses are flooded. I meander, I smell, and look deeply into my environment. I pause and ponder that which I find interesting. I begin to bury my nose in a cool running stream and drink the crisp water there in; delicious and satisfying. Quenching my thirst is something I never will forget. What a sensation, it's powerful to be contented with water. Now and then I just sit, looking around me. The scene somehow enters me and I feel as if I and the expanse are not separate; not two different things but one thing of peace. I look so deeply at a dark green maple leaf, I see into it, deep inside of it, yet it's so thin. There is a chain of worlds inside that leaf, it's mesmerizing. I smell a pine cone and marvel at the pointed yet rounded lip of each shingle like protrusion. The cone is a matrix of beauty and balance. It is almost vibrating and at the same time perfectly still.

All of this makes me contemplate where and what I am. How did I find the cave to begin with? How did I awaken, and why and how long was my hibernation? I have no recollection of these answers. Maybe I can find them along my journey into the expanse. I am alone as I travel, I like it. I begin to enter rolling hills and foothills of the mountain terrain. I roll and somersault for fun, down a gully of tall windy grasses. I cover some distance and at one shocking moment a sound hits me. It's a bell-like drum in my ears and in this moment I realize I don't know where the cave is anymore. I tremble and freeze, and soon have no choice but to accept this. I may be able to recover my path back there. But I am uncertain and want to eat. I move on, and lead my mind back to a comfortable curiosity around the next hillside. A taste is on my tongue, and it's been there from the start, only I just now became aware of it. It's powdery and dusty and is like the taste of moths in my mouth. I remember this but don't know from when or where. The taste of moth wings, it motivates me to replace it with something new. I seek nutrient and food.

I move on, I survey, seeking food but of what nature I am wondering. I feel the warmth on my back and it feels good and hear light rhythmic winds gradually getting louder which means it's getting closer. I pause and turn and a large and bold bird lands above me on a branch. He twitches and looks directly at me and still sees all around us. His eyes are pools of black obsidian. He questions me mentally and points both North and South four times. Nudging a response from me, I greet him with honor and respect for he can fly high and see well beyond. He must see far, far to the North as well as to the South. He begins to speak to me and asks, "Who are?", and then hops up higher to branches above before finishing. I have every intention of conversing but he looks North and South again and in a flash he's gone. I turn and feel jolted to my core as a prodding stick pokes my side and calmly says, "Who are you, from whence have you come"?

I turn startled, to see a tall man carrying a staff pointed at me. He is covered by the brim of a round hat blocking the light that would befall his features. He is bearded, and all I can see are his eyes, or more the shape of his eyes. They are so female and strange but his figure is masculine and the beard is male for sure.

His voice is low and rumbling but not aggressive. He is not threatening but asks again. "Who are you, and from whence have you come?"

I answer immediately "My name is Little King Bear", but don't know how this name came out of me. I don't know how I knew my name. I traveled from the cave, I awoke there in the darkness and now I am here. "Where is here?" I ask.

The bearded man responds, "Well you are neither here nor there and yet you are here, always. You came from the darkness of the cave and are you sure you did not come from the cave of light?"

I reply, "I awoke in darkness and fell upon the light as I wandered to the opening and in the light I see so many things but where is here, where am I and from where did you arrive?"

He said "You are here, and here is by design as you have made it. Do you not remember your first thoughts? They are as you have intended and you're welcome. I am here as I always have been and will remain. You know not my vibratory note, but you will indeed as you move further from the cave. I am on my way up into those high hills there (he pointed with his staff), you will travel on Little King Bear…Doksha!"

"What is doksha?" I asked.

"An ancient tongue of the Lakota people, It means until we meet again". He turned and his back and a cloak is all I saw as he moved swiftly away.

He was leaving so fast I am compelled to say something to continue the talking but I can only say, "Wait, wait!"

Then I feel a rumble. It is his voice but he does not turn back to face me. With the sound clear in my ears, yet he is fading in the distance, "Be wary of words of passing tongues, for knowledge is a frightening affair." He was gone.

I pause and decide to put foot in front of foot and move along but in my pause, I feel a stillness as I think about the encounter, about his words and their vibration. I want to heed his words as I detect they were wise and meaningful but I am stuck. His words are from a stranger, a passing tongue and he himself says to be wary of such. I wonder and ponder, then move on. The sun is setting in the west, I head east. Finding a chalice, a small wooden bowl in the roots of huge oak tree I bed down for evening and the moon is upon me. I am hungry, and chew a pine needle for taste, to remove the moths in my mouth. I stare at the bowl but it is empty. Pine is good, but still I am hungry. I breathe out and in my exhale; I awaken from what seems like an eternity.

Lying in bed, I stretch my ribs and legs to move my feet on the floor. Put gravity into vertical motion I feel the weight of my body as I walk across the *Tiny Yellow Kingdom* (my endearing name for my studio home). It's yellow from the street outside. I live in a small dwelling where I can shut out most of the outside world and be in peace and work out my reflections. I am on the coast, a pleasant climate to boot. I get up, make coffee, and sit in a way on the floor where I can stretch my lower back while still enjoying my morning cup. A gesture from the cup reminds of the wooden bowl. In this I realize I was just dreaming. So I recount the man with beard, the large bird, the cave and so on. It was so complex and full of detail. I was lucid in the dream. I was aware enough to think and make decisions, so I know I was lucid. I remember it all and now know I was in the specific state of mind known as the nagual by the Toltecs. I've been reading the Toltec teachings and Carlos Castaneda, on and off for years. The nagual in the terms of the Toltec is that part of our awareness that is watching ourselves when in the light of the moon (meaning the night/dream). So as we sleep and dream, we shift into the nagual which, if we are conscious of it, is the part of ourselves that is infinite, the part that is aware of our spirit. Conversely the part of us that is watching ourselves in the light of the sun (everyday life when mind is going outward) is called the tonal. Tonal means sun.

The Toltecs practice the art of dreaming, which is a way of grooming conscious and personal power when we dream. The power we gain in the dream affects the tonal or waking life. The power wielded in the dream can be wielded in the waking reality by the shifts in awareness in both worlds. To be a master at dreaming is to be a nagual. One is so aware of the infinite self that he can attain total freedom, even from death. Many cultures in the Americas have similar systems of shifting awareness or moving toward enlightenment. All over Mexico, Central America, Bolivia, and Peru, these ideas and philosophies permeate their spirituality.

I sip the warmth of the morning and remember ancient sun worshiping ideas of how humans are divine rays of the sun (the power source of all life in our solar system). They were much more intelligent than most people think. The mapping of the system and the effects of the sun, solar winds, solar flares and the power of light manifesting/growing matter is sacred knowledge to them. I believe all lasting and great civilizations were sun worshipers. They knew its sacred power and encoded it into art, architecture, myth and language in ways we today are still discovering.

The sun rotates on its axis every 27 days (31 days at the poles); this generates and regulates fertility cycles in humans. Women menstruate on the same cycle. Spinning at the equator at a different rate than at its poles, the sun's equator has a wave-like wobble, that fans out radiation particles in a rhythm of 4 pulses per rotation. So the sun sort of has four sides as it spins. This is called the sunspot cycle in modern science. These particles are like a water sprinkler causing arms of particles to fling out, and this is what the ancient symbol the swastika depicts, as well as many other armed symbols of the sun.

These sunspot cycles, as well as the sunlight radiation, have a massive impact on man's conscious and spiritual ascension. See, the ascension of man's soul to heaven is the process of taking the light ray that you are and reversing the manifestation into matter (the body). We go from matter back into light or spirit consciousness. The light of the sun causes all life on Earth to exist. It is said in many spiritual texts that God is light. Without the light of the sun all life will cease on Earth. Man is said to be the measure of all things, and so it goes that man is this because he is the individualized soul (sol, sun) of God/light. We ascend through a very lengthy and complex process but it involves raising consciousness away from matter (the body and senses) and returning it to super-consciousness (light consciousness). Our soul is individualized spirit; our body is personality of the soul. Personality or the word *persona* means mask, so our personality is a mask. It is not our true essence; it is an expression of our material form. Our spirit form is the light itself.

The return to spirit is how to get to heaven and doing so is how to escape hell ...when we die. As we move consciousness into higher states (through the chakras), we increase our electromagnetic voltage. The sun's light is split into electric (masculine) and magnetic (feminine) to manifest all the frequency wavelengths of vibratory matter. Increasing the voltage of the soul moves it further and further away from its material home in the body. As the soul gets closer to spirit, it sheds the body and has the potential to become one with God-spirit, depending on it voltage. The increase of voltage is done by love. Love is the growing and evolutionary force in the universe, and causes a glow or halo of light in the heart and in the material body as well. This is why enlightened, awakened, or anointed beings are always depicted with light halos around them. Halo comes from the Greek word helios, meaning light of the sun. If we are pure, we will increase our voltage, and when the body dies the energy of the soul can escape the gravity of Earth and become one with God. If the voltage is not high enough, the energy of the soul will resonate with genes of similar frequency and reincarnate again on the material plane or Earth plane. By design humans cannot live on other planets, our energetic mold is linked to Earth and Earth alone for it is the matter ground for the ascension process for humans. After returning to spirit, the energy may transform into other worlds, planets, or dimensions as spirit designs it. But humans spring from Earth as apples from apple trees. Still our origins are cosmic in the light of God.

Each incarnation gives us the opportunity to grow our halo, increase our light, increase or love. Our love gets bigger and bigger as we learn to love others and ourselves. All the ascended masters teach to love your neighbor as yourself in order to brighten your light and raise your consciousness to super-consciousness. Tesla shows us that electricity bends light, so in order for us to escape the material world's density, we truly have to change our vibration, our light frequency, to such intensity that density cannot bend or hold us any longer. We as spirit, transcend time-space and space-time. He also shows us the principle of motion, (energy can be transformed into matter and vice versa). So energy moves across the equation into matter and so they equal each other. As above (in the heavens), so below (our bodies in the world of matter).

Before I breach the door to the worlds abound, I have a flashback to another dream I had in the night; so strange and deeply saddening. I have no feeling as to why it feels the way it does. I know now that this is the second time I have dreamt about infant baby girls and they are more than normal dreams, they are vivid, participatory and lucid. Always a group is pursuing me but I am always aware of them, so always cunning and ahead of them. They don't know quite how to find me, I like it this way. It's tense and I see that I must cross a small canal. The water is lake green, the banks are grassy. I see a small boat perched in the middle of the canal. I ooze into the water and quietly move across. As I move through the water, I naturally grab the boat for a rest and a place to pause. Peering over the bow I see three tiny baby girls sitting upright, legs crossed like mummies. The boat has three flat ribs wide enough for a seat. One girl is sitting on the middle rib and two are sitting on the back rib. I only look at the one closest to me, I see her so closely, so fragile. I know the other girls are there but I never really look at them. They are out of my focus, in the periphery. I see her toothless little eyes and mouth. She is dying. I feel the deepest pain and sorrow in my heart and abdomen. The more I see her, the more I ache. She is tiny, helpless, and about to die. I reach for her, hold her. I am still in the water. I swim her across the canal, struggling. I reach the wet long grassy bank and rest as I gently hold her and look into her eyes. My heart aches in so much pain; my throat migrates up into my head with tears as I see she is dying. I cry in terrible agony and hold her as she lies on the cold, grassy, earth. Before she passes, I wake.

As I said, this is the second dream like this. The first is similar. I am in an urban area walking with a badly beaten baby girl. She is in my arms bleeding into my jacket and clothes. I am desperately calling out for help. Please someone help me. I call out but there is no one, no one around. She has been beaten and her face is badly disfigured, mostly on her right side. I feel so helpless and full of anguish. Who is she, who is this baby girl? Maybe a soul relative. Maybe my mother's miscarriage before I was born. I am unsure. It rattles me to have such deep sad emotions and even in my waking state these feelings are there.

I am now off to go about my day, in the light of the sun, the tonal. Out of bed, stretching and enjoying a warm cup of coffee. I head out to work, the day's duties, and then look forward to time on a little ranch where the wind blows through the trees and sings a song of calmness and healing and peace.

As I unfold the day, I have moments of hearing the voice of the man in my dream. It's not as if he is actually speaking to me, it's just my memory of his presence. He had a weight I could feel, it was like some sort of energetic signature. Things he said to me came through during my day but I couldn't recall him saying them until I heard them again in my head. When they bubbled up I knew it was not the first time I had heard them, they were all familiar. He told me he was a part of the etheric fabric known as the imaginatrix and that it was the creator of the matrix we all agree to call nature. He said nature is real but a much more dense vibratory state than the imaginatrix from which it comes. It is hidden from the ordinary person's awareness, and this is what make ordinary awareness ordinary and in the open view. Deeper lies the crack between worlds, or where worlds begin to differentiate from a unified source.

He said, "certain exceptional humans have been hunting this knowledge for eons, then cataloging it in hopes of retaining and passing this special knowledge down the generations. However, it has been lost and obscured many times by unforeseeable consequences. Still, there are those shamans and warriors of knowledge that find the crack and peer in with their intended awareness. All dream potentials exist there and it's vast, beyond mental boundaries, and more importantly it is where all technology originates for man. From this original technology, man realizes that all technologies spring forth from himself, he is the point of origin."

I shook my head and shivered, I was barely able to conceive of the meaning of his words.

He went on; "It is timeless, and very few laws function there. The only laws are the laws of creative boundlessness, so its limits are those that the imagination sets in place in the now. It is where, reality, insanity, and identity dissolves into mystery. The word of being and the image of forms and archetypes all open the way through this imaginatrix. There is a caveat though; the law upholds the boundlessness of creativity but self-loathing, hate, and what men call evil, fizzle out in this dimension. By design, hate has within itself its own loss of inertia or force, so it is short lived. Simply put, it destroys itself, and that is its nature. The word, logos, and I-dea have influence from and in the imaginatrix. Some peoples just call it the spirit world. Wise men have imported their intentions from the unconscious meeting in their dream state (from the imaginatrix) and then figured out how to move with it while conscious (in the waking state). This means that the spirit world is in fact real and the spirits within exist in our super-consciousness and they ebb and flow, to and fro. They are intimately a part and linked to us but we have no control over when they decide to come through. When they appear or arrive, we do at that time have some influence over them. The reason why we have no control over them when they are in the super-consciousness is because the super-consciousness is a vibrating, universal world that is not unique to any one person. It is universal to all people and the spirits can appear to you based on your mind mold, your psychological mold. They dress and dance for you based on your deep seated cultural and soul rhythms.

We do have connection and influence with them and just like you can lucidly change and create your dream elements you can interact with the spirits in the spirit world. But be keenly aware that man still cannot make the dreaming state appear, he himself does not cause it, he finds himself folded in it. The dreaming state created by the imaginatrix or universal unconscious decides independently on its own volition when to be. You cannot make yourself dream, the dream appears on its own, filled with the condensations of light we know as spirits. You cannot make yourself dream but you can work with and create imprints upon your soul during sleep. This is something we've lost, the awareness and purpose for sleep. The soul dis-identified with the physical body during sleep, it does so to integrate the universe with the being. Waking consciousness is the integrating of the body to the material reality. Both are needed to evolve the soul as well as the universe at large.

In sleep, if trained properly, humans can imprint their souls with their creative intent. They can also discover the organization and patterns of nature and the universe. This has implications in the waking reality also. We can work out solutions to life by slipping between the veils of waking and slumber. Visions spontaneously occur to direct souls progress and evolutionary plateaus. There is an alchemical dew that enriches vitality and fortitude in the beings, which only occurs in sleep. It is purposed just as morning dew upon the plants, it is not a decoration. Within the potent condensation falling upon the leafy beings is contained the light and sound harmonic of the planets and the cosmos of that particular night. The awareness and working with this dew offers us the plant and us the encoded message of our own will to power of spiritual ascension and evolution. If we but, get out of our material body and see the subtleties of how we humans came to being, we will become aware that all manifestation is primarily powered by the unseen force that energetically builds the spiraling geometries of material. Like most things in the modern man, he has foolishly strayed from or removed the sacred within it.

Think, how the gaseous elements of oxygen and nitrogen and such are so intrinsically related to the consciousness of people. Oxygen, like mind, is subtle and invisible, yet still absolutely infused in the building of human life and consciousness. The stress of the human body is so linked to thought, mind, gas, and chemistry, as it unfolds the life force it carries through a lifetime. Psychophysiology, or the nature and nurture, work together, pinging back and forth and not in an arbitrary way. The relationship of environment to body is malleable and works in harmony. We humans are not manifesting here on earth as a victim or arbitrarily. We are deeply a key part of the architecture of both inner and outer realities and when this realization no longer sleeps in you, you discover you are awake, deeply in the self. Empowerment appears directly from the navel of yourself. The dew of the cosmic being falls upon the pedals of the human soul, this is not coincidence, it is the coherence of magical design.

We can sweetly call upon the archetypes and covenants in heartfelt song, but it is still them who decide whether or not to answer. The burning bushes, sacred rowan trees of life and knowledge, the yogi, and the ascended masters of light, the thunder beings, the bird tribe, the star people, and the eagle's emanations are all there and here deciding for themselves to bio-dynamically live, die, and manifest. Nature only reveals her unity to the mind searching for its own unification.

2

History Mystery

history is what you've been told, it's his-story. Mystery is what you unfold, it's yours. Re-connect to your psyche, and unpack what is and has occurred there within, this will lead to unity. First just acknowledge that most men have lost the awareness of the psychophysical relationship, and this is why we are cowering from feeling the world within us. Western man has been conditioned to accept his own spiritual enslavement and in his lethargy now welcomes the slave driver to bring him his traditions and rituals just as if his morning slop trough is being filled. The problem here is obvious; the enslaved will eat whatever is brought to him. This serves to further enslave himself in his own act of giving away of his sovereign mind and soul. It becomes the mode of conditioning to numb and pacify when asked to be still and feel what it is naturally to be a human. Very few have the warrior spirit and passion in their heart to feel the truth. They would much rather run from feeling and dive deep into fragmented oblivion. The history tellers only tell you what they want you to know, and then the sheep seek the shepherd and slaughter.

I was given by Thot a few jumping points to study, these were little pebbles of idea he knew would send me with the curiosity of wind, sailing to connect the dots of alternate history. He said that this is just a few bold historical smudges and once I figured them out, it would become easier to see others if I chose to look. I picked up threads and followed them, and started with the pebble of the east to west movement of culture across Europe, instead of the west to east teaching. In Orkney Scotland, the small island burial homes of Skara Brae have been unearthed and were found to be built in the same cosmological pattern as the homes of the Dogon people of West Africa. Scotland itself received its name from the Irish conquerors and settlers but they are referring to an African princess. Why was I not taught this in school? Scotland was named in reverence to the term of endearment given to the daughter of the 4th century king Menes of Egypt. She was called Scota and the king is buried in Ireland to this day. He and she were honored and intrinsically connected to the land of the druids, Ireland, Britain, and Scotland, but why? An African princess named the Scottish land, but was she dark skinned and of African descent? The connection is alive and now we see how the culture of the Dogon appeared in the homes and architecture of the Scottish of Skara Brae, they shared cosmological and cultural beliefs. They may have different bloodlines but were initiated into the same colleges of higher knowledge and this is why their structures are built using the same cosmological signatures.

It may be said by some scholars that the Dogon people gave rise to pharaonic Egypt based on their cultural similarities and stories. This is all before 18th dynasty Egypt was corrupted and purchased by outsiders. There is an ancient language spoken in northern Scotland called Faroese and is linguistically unrelated to the other Scottish tongues. It's called Faroese (pharaohs) because it was the tongue of the original Dogon pharaohs and assimilated by the schools of the druids. Pharaoh originally referred to a place or region, and then became stuck to the people who used it and eventually became a title for those people. Pharaoh people were higher minded people who embodied fa-Ra (father -ra) phar-oh, the keepers of sacred knowledge.

In Dogon civilization eight people were selected to be initiated into the schools of knowledge. These eight once encoded with sacred knowledge would systematically impart it on others who were pure of intention and this is how small kingdoms and kings became civilisations. The knowledge was not exclusive but was not easy to obtain, so only those who asked the right questions recursively were deemed to hold it. They chose the eight people symbolically by the scientific process of mitosis, which they say they were given by non-human star people. The drawings and oral traditions confirm they knew of genetics and creation cell division thousands of years before western science. These star people they name the Nommo and their descendants are called the Ari which spread throughout the west and are now called the Aryan. They are not a race, the Aryan are people educated in schools of sacred knowledge, and this sacredness the Dogon still carry and protect today.

It is said the Ari spread and started 4 or 5 kingdoms, these being Peru, China, Ireland, Egypt, and India. These started as agricultural kingships and held the knowledge of the cycles of nature to flourish crops and peoples. These sacred cycles were taught by the ARI/ARU to propagate the health of populations. Many similar origin myths are held in these cultures today. The Vedic texts begin in the Bhagavad Gita as having spiritual knowledge imparted on them by the Aryans. So now we know the ancient name for Orkney is ARU, a derivative of ARI. It continues. a-Pe-Te-e are phonetic values in Egyptian for the 4 aspects on sunlight known as ATUM. In Egypt the great Hermes Trismegistus states his philosophy that all is ATUM. These 4 aspects give rise to the eternal symbol of the solar cross, which is found by all agricultural kingdoms worldwide. The modern Christians adopted this pagan symbol for their own solar cult.

The solar cross is more than a symbol; it embodies the time movements and tracking of the solar year for growing crops and planting the flooded river. It's no coincidence that the English word year is derived from the solar symbol. The word Year was once spelled yeah, which was in turn shorted to yes. Yes is Hebrew for fire-light or sun. We see the full circle. The four aspects also represent sun rise, sun set, and sun solstices. These are equinoxial, upper and lower Egypt, and are the solstices. Ta is an unplowed field, Ra is a planted field, Pa is a granary, and Er is the growing crop. These four aspects of light became embodiments of cosmic principles and the peoples of this sacred knowledge used them to harmonically balance with nature. They did not fall into the trap of personality worship. This is why the druids, gauls, Dogon, shemsu-hor and other earth keepers were purposefully killed by jealous and corrupted atonists who cannot feel their own putrid heart. These nasty elitists, set themselves up as ruling royalty and so separated are they from God; they seek to divide all others who will give their sovereignty to them in enslavement.

These are the people who tell you your history. I began to see, their same tactics under different flags throughout the histories of the world. They show up everywhere there is genocide and population control and they easily spin media events because they own nearly all outlets of media. They will pacify you with the illusion of truth, honesty, and sweep your emotions into a steady tornado of anxiety. "Tyranny is always more organized than freedom." (Charles Peguy)

So why is this important, to know that our version of history is a half told, half-truth? If you are asking this question, the answer couldn't be clearer; to reveal the precipice of false stories you've been basing your cultural, spiritual, psychic, and emotional approaches to yourself on. Walk to the social hall proudly displaying your orthodox double cross upon your breast without a clue that the vaticus templars are laughingly boasting as you wear the slave seal of your own double crossing, which they handed to you with poisonous smiles. It is important to do the discerning work that can only be found deep within each person's own history and see it in reality. Set it straight, become the feeling of a whole human being. This can only be done in harmony with nature, the cosmos, and our reflected self in the macrocosm. First know that the evil in the world is of man and of maneuvers of deception. Whenever you spot deception, you know it's a move of separation and seeks to divide you. If your approach to reality harmonizes with nature's order you will be starting from wholeness (holiness) and division will disappear.

The evildoers will have their hell all to themselves, while nature will call her children back to her in peace and unity. As Plato explains, "God who knows the beginning, the middle, and the end of all that is, advances in a straight course according to nature; justice follows the transgressor, and he who is happy follows the divine law closely and humbly."

One afternoon we spoke of my research. Thot reminded me of the cause of such tyranny among men. He said, man in his original being was at peace and due to natural shifts in the earth, he had to face cataclysms and floods and harsh conditions. Man became afraid of such events but learned to harmonize with them by keeping his spirit and mind intently listening to the mother goddess. After the last diluvian floods, men selfishly sought kingdom for themselves for fear of loss from future disasters. In doing so, these men perpetuated the lie that the sky is falling, and through children of new generations taught a psychic fear.

Then through creation of hierarchy and hoarding worldly power, they set themselves up to propagandize a system of ancestral trauma. Once people became fearful and afflicted, a stream of continual psychic trauma was taught to their own children by themselves without them even being aware of it. Parents slowly became more and more fragmented by the news of the day (which is controlled, created, and funded by the corrupt tyrants) they built up dependency on the hierarchy of power to save them.

The saviors were the destroyers dressed in the garb of a woolly king, god, or pharaoh. Over time and generation, people fashioned an idealized self-image, a pseudo self and began to live in this part of their mind. This is a trauma bound ego pain loop. With time, they became accepting of their mental and sometimes physical enslavement and historical amnesia develops; this is when people have forgotten their own true and natural history of the divine essence within. They then believe whatever HIS-STORY they are told and will war with themselves and nature too. Thot, rattled his head with his knuckles, leaned into me with a piercing stare, and said, this is why history is important! Man must stop living inauthentically, stop avoiding his subconscious shadow and dive into his anxiety, for deep in there are the shattered pieces of the mirror of conscious wholeness. Be wary of social collectivism, all men are their own selfhood, king, queen, and savior. If need be, it's fine to lean on and support your fellow man but you cannot ever climb the mountain with another man's feet.

Looking into the origins of religious text, I uncovered the many traditions which gave birth to the bible. In this collection the godhead is always identified as the tree in the garden. God speaks through the tree and is the creator of the woman. Be that, the female is the first form created and the male is placed in her womb by the merging conception of god and woman. Now see the twisting of physiological thought to say woman if born of the rib of a man, this is not only counter to what exists in nature (which is god) but an attempt to subvert the natural, lie. The tree is the universal symbol of cosmic natural intelligence and is seen in modern traditions of ascended masters attaining enlightenment under the tree. Images of Buddha, Herne, Hermes, Tenuti, Enki, Jesus, Babaji, Merlin, Moses, Confucius, are all symbolically placed under the tree. The tree of life in nature is the tree of life within the body, the branching nazareth cerebro-spinal system.

The female (Eve) is always found connected or close to the tree because this is the symbolic language used to inform that she is intimately connected to the icon of higher nature intelligence (the tree). Elohim (elm tree), Yahweh/yhwh (yew tree), Moses which is a title not a name (burning bush or tree). Adonis, Romulus, Krishna, Dionysus, Glycon, Zoroaster (zo-Ra-star), Attis, Horus are all born of the female alone and have no father. The Adam, Atum, Atom character is thus the offspring of the union between god and woman. In the Nag hammadi texts of Egypt Adam born of Eve, thus the goddess Sophia descends to earth to banish the seven landlords out of Eden, these being the elohim. Knowing the temple of God is the human body, the notion of higher intelligence, the tree, is planted within. Its branches, the cerebral spine where the serpent (sine wave serpent) energetically flows within the body of spiraling enfolded consciousness. The word cerebrospinal etymologically means cere or Sara/ brahim which is Sara and Abraham the male and female genders united in spin or spiral.

The physical representation, the spine, is the connection between the human (physical) and unconscious (spirit). When physical injuries and blockages affect the spine they affect the physical and spiritual... (The branching tree is the spiraling serpent of gender or generation, within the human spine. The scepter of power and wisdom. Sept-or means seven fold which is the branching tree to eternal wisdom.)

The branching of the tree is obviously replicated in nature on Earth as well as in the universe. Branching, which means dividing or splitting, is the way of nature from a cellular level to a universal level and replicates itself in all things. The Latin word for branching is ramosa –Ram (Ra), osa (full of). The word tree, meaning druid, durable, or duration, the everlasting myriad of branching.

Man and woman in spiritual histories, become anointed

through initiation into the mysteries (my story); the true story within, the knowing of how to move from the center of being. This anointing is the healthy oil in the spine formed of the marriage of pituitary and pineal secretions. These same iconic symbols of man, woman, tree, garden, paradise, serpent are uniformly common across the ancient world, why? The answer is, all these cultures were teaching and practicing syncratic knowledge of the self. This is also why so many ancient megalithic monuments are coordinated with the stars. They are the ancient science, which we should know and understand.

In the western tradition, the problems of corruption are traced back to the time of Akhenaten, who propagandized by the mainstream media, is painted as beneficent. Deep research reveals another truth about him. His family culture of Hyksos pharaohs were persuaded to disseminate the worship of the deity named Aton. He also, forced all citizens to only worship Aton by rule of law. Certain wealthy families bought the religion and forced it down the throats of citizens by way of politics. Akhenaten caused rebellion among the people and was eventually impeached and forced out of Egypt as the tyrannical icon of atonism. It's a long trail to trace but be it known that his descendants and their families are still selling the same brimstone fear media today. They seek wealth and power at any cost, and have no love in their hearts. Living a life of wicked self-mutilation, they seek to force any type of separation and enslavement on all others and they are sadistic pope merchants that have been writing the western history for centuries. The time has come to awaken to the truth within, and listen to the voice of the mighty rebel who comes with his teaching of love to reclaim unity consciousness and reveal that separatist mentality breeds illusion.

These families in roman terms are known as the Piso, Flavian, and Julian families but they stem from the 13th dynasty century invaders of previous times in Egypt. These invaders are the Hyksos who set themselves up as royal dynasties and took over the seat of the pharaoh with Akhenaten. They ruled through priesthoods and religious psychologies, and once forced out of Egypt, they began to write their story as if they were the good slaves with moral hearts but this is farcical. They control the history by powerful wealth and distribution of media. One obvious lie they've told, is that of being poor slaves when they left Egypt, but they left with horses, camels, and supplies and in those times this meant wealth, lots of wealth. Slaves were not privy to owning livestock or abundant supplies.

More unfolds with the creation of spin off religions of the Jews and their father Abraham. The story is given by themselves, the deceivers, the atonist. They say that Abraham was a wanderer, knowing no one and having no relations in upper Egypt. Yet shortly after arriving into the cities he became liked and promoted to the father of the religion's theocracy, he was second in power to the pharaoh. How could this be? A poor wanderer of a foreign land walking into and becoming the ruler of an entire nation. The research I have found shows that he arrived in a large mob of shepherd kings known as the Hyksos, they had wealth and power and were vicious marauders who worship the dark forces. And these tyrannical families moved through history by writing it themselves, controlling it. Today you can see their symbols all over Rome and London and America. The obelisks marking their graves across royal elite gravesites are revealing markers of who they are. Most Europeans use a tombstone or stone plates to honor their dead but these royals trace their bloodlines back to Dynastic Egypt and so mark their dead with twisted symbols of the corrupted pharaoh. A thousand years later they went back into Egypt to conquer and destroy as much of the tombs and temples as they could in order to hide traces of the real story.

In modern times the queen of England still heralds Egyptian symbols in all rituals and ceremony. She even states that she rules her seat in the name of the house of David. Well who is David? The word is in origin not a name, but is a title. The David or dovid is the general or commander. These royal elites and she are blatantly telling their rulership is by war command and tyranny. And of course their mode of operation is subversion, lies and division. These symbols are so pervasive they show up in the District of Columbia in monuments and obelisks. The Star of David is printed on the back of every seat in the American congress, why? Let's ask why this particular symbol, why not any other? And the western corporation of America is ruled and dictated by the Roman pope who funds and controls all the wealth. And the hidden hand that Rome answers to is known as the Jesuit order, they being the black pope so to speak. These are all the sun cult of Aton, and there are many families and secret societies linked in between.

An importance shall be placed on the power of wielding the magic wand of the mighty pen. When these families posing as gods, kings, queens, and pharaohs handed us the simulacra version of history they use terms and symbols from inside their own halls. They give these talismanic words to the public who are taught alternate meanings, while all along the writers of the words encode and know their secret meaning that is only for them. This is secret deception and keeps them separate from us, keeps them in power and you as the chattel—citizen, birth- certified stock who know not the difference, and even begs them for merit and status.

It continues and goes on and on and is seen in the written histories of America. Just one such story to ponder is the war for American independence from England. Pause, think and ask how all these immigrants found the funds to travel the Great Atlantic Ocean in ships and build the wealthy new land? Every ship and shipment was a business transaction funded by these same royal elite families who chuckle as they sell the public the idea that they fought the monarchy of England, overthrew them, and won without a dime of their own. All this supposedly done on the backs of starving poor immigrants. Where did the bullets, uniforms, guns all come from? Possibly the Hudson Bay Company of England? It's obvious, the story was orchestrated, written, and played out and fully bank backed by the writers of official history.

Now, gaining a deep grasp of the power of the pen in history, I began to study myths and their origins, their earliest meanings and versions. When diving deep in this well, huge shifts occur as you learn how to read and understand symbols from multiple layers. Here is some history to question about the Adam/Eve story. Concerning its meaning with numbers, how number symbolism tells the myth. Start with the names. Adam means atom (indivisible unit) or ONE (1), and Eve being even balances by being two (2) or evenly divisible. Adam=1 and Eve=2 in occult number theory. The odd numbers are all masculine and the even are feminine.

The number one was the first manifested number. It's called the reducible one. The reason why it's reducible is because it has a body, so manifestation occurs. Even conceptually it has a body. But what manifested the one has many names. You can call it the void, infinite power, the ground of being and so on. It is called the irreducible one, the one that cannot be divided. The reason it cannot be divided is because it has no manifestation, so it has no body. The only thing in the universe that has no body or is infinite, is the universe itself. It cannot be divided or reduced and so all existing bodies eventually dissolve into it. Everything else, on some level has some sort of container or body and can be divided or split. So there is really only one thing in the universe that is truly infinite which is the universe itself. All other bodies can be divided or split. So the number 1 is the reducible one, its creator is the irreducible one.

Out of one, it created or replicated itself and this is the way photons work. Photons are interesting, you can call them cells and these cells regenerate themselves by splitting themselves and basically creating a clone or replica. And photons, as far as we know have no volume or mass which means, from a photon's perspective (anywhere in the universe) there is no space or time, and may not really be bound by form at all. The concept of a quantum is a sensed anomaly but has never been held or seen to actually have a form. It is highly likely that particles really have no body or shell and are more like a resonance than an object. They replicate themselves or birth themselves at the speed of light. They are constantly birthing or procreating themselves. And so the way in which I understand man in numerical terms is we have the divine essence of God and the infinite universe within us, however we are not its original creator. We are only a procreator so we've been given the power, the awareness, the will, the intent to co-create reality or create our own reality. This is a procreative process describing the number one.

The number two is that process (one) duplicating itself and coming together in a union. This is where female energy is born and so all the odd numbers are said to be masculine and direct and electric and imbalanced for a reason, while all the even (which is where we get the word Eve) numbers are said to be feminine or curved and magnetic and balancing. For this reason she is designed to balance out the 1 and she can do this because she is able to divide/reduce herself evenly. So 1/1 is 2, evenly divided. So the numbers 2, 4, 6, 8 and so on, can always be divided evenly in a perfect balance or unity. This is how the universe, in numerical terms, makes all manifested bodies come into existence and so we use numbers as the universal scientific language to display this.

Simply from duality (Eve) coming into existence, combined with the reducible one (Adam), automatically creates trinity or a third philosophical concept. The two of them working together create something new, something metaphysical or spiritual. Here trinity comes in. The three aspects create the geometric triangle which orientated upward calls into being the male phallus and when oriented downward calls into being the female vagina or womb. Combine the two opposing trinities into the six pointed star and balance, union, birth, and creation continues ever new.

This process continues through 4 (the sacred directions of N,S,E,W), 5, 6, and so on until the number 9 (the number of completion). Nine manifests the sacred hoops, cycles, and spirals right to the core of being. Here in this awareness, we dance the days away and a sun is born.

Thot, spoke intently. He remained intense and

devilishly focused. He said, "remember that the fractals of light require inherent resistance for growth. The resistance is a kind of barrier to life. It is a relentless barrage of challenge, a force calling or reckoning us to freedom, freedom from tyranny and annihilation. There are dark magicians who use technologies combined with materialism to destroy the human body. Through biological chips, nanocomputers, and oppressive surveillance they seek to erode the fundamentals of soul incarnation. The human body being the temple, provides souls a means to incarnate the individualized spirit into a dense light form. This density light form (body) offers souls the incarnation and reincarnation process so it may consciously learn the maneuver of immortality.

These dark magicians aim to destroy or alter the body so as to hinder or stop the soul's evolution. It wears down the health body so a soul may have no divine form in which to incarnate into. The soul requires a body that is attuned and aware to the natural solar and earthly rhythms. The soul and divine human form are both rhythmic clusters of divine light. When a body is aware of the natural solar harmonies, we call this health. Be not afraid of the darkness in these magicians, as fearfulness is the syndrome they wish to pervert and control the soul with. The process of awakening, if engaged in wholeheartedly shatters the childish game they play upon it. It is important when facing a devious enemy, not to accept the weapons he offers you in which to fight him. Know thyself, make keen decisions not from his repertoire of possible choices, but from within your own center self. Here total freedom and truth, guide you beyond the trappings of the unenlightened."

3

Language, Writing
and Alternate History

The more I study the esoteric and spiritual nature
of things and myself, I find the hidden
connection of meaning, words, numbers, and
culture. I feel we are all walking up an allegorical mountain
and even as we walk together our steps and strides are
unique. We may walk the entire way with another on our
side or we may never see the others traversing the alternate
routes and ridges. When we arrive at the summit and look at
the view upwards, we are held in the natural majesty of
nature. We climb, and then look at our steps along the path
to the top and see each foot print. It all becomes clear that
our companions' footprints be next to ours, they still created
a different path to the top. They, like us, walked their own
journey and still arrived in the light of the sun or heavens.
Religions are like this, and as we see deeply into them we
realize they are maps up the great mountain, simple guides
and are helpful, but not worth fighting over, as we all have

the truth of the inner compass molded into our unique design. If we become so dependent upon the so called experts, and teachers of the society dictated norm, we slowly divorce ourselves from our own central compass. Then over time, people tend to perpetuate escapism from reality and thus only live on the periphery of their own being. These people often live unknowingly disconnected from their deeper emotions and have no voice. Sadly, these are our neighbors programed by the masters of media. The opposite is possible as well, and I call out to people of the earth to courageously challenge the status quo and remember the intrinsic value of total freedom. Without it, a puppet is all that remains. All these words are my own syncretic collection of truths. Don't believe them; verify them for and by your own self. Sovereign beings we are.

Languages can be a bit slippery and tricky but we must agree on a common method in order to communicate. This is the word and its power. As we grunt along our emotions, the expressions hit tones that humans are built to understand and as we become better communicators the more refined our expressions become. As ancient languages moved across the globe they morphed into new word variations but still hold the root tones and their meaning. So we will explore some of this process. Egypt, Sumer, and other ancient culture used pictures or symbols to communicate words and meaning. The symbol or glyph is extremely effective because a picture is encoded with layers of meaning and words. A picture is worth a thousand words.

I find myself devouring books, symbols, and writing. As I retire at night, I read in bed, a cozy situation that brings me deep meditation. I fall into a deep sleep and see a shimmering dragon glide across the dark star lit sky. It covers the entire sky and moves over me towards the west. I know he sees me but he is not attacking, he is just presenting his majesty and power as if with a message of some sort. In slumber, I am standing out in the cold of night and Thot appears beside me. He looks over at me and nudges me with his eyes as if to welcome me in some strange way.

He breathes in audibly and without looking at me he says, "you have so much to learn, better get started".

I didn't respond but knew he was correct.

He said, "the cold will keep you alert, so stand or sit but get comfortable". He began to speak of ancient times. He said, "within the word you'll find roots and tones with eons of meaning. Following the movement of the word and its morphology and history reveals itself within the corruption of men (the conquers who held the pen). Keen discernment is necessary!

What I tell you is truth, but you may have a hard time believing it as your culture refuses to part with its psychopathic self-importance. If you learn to see as seers do, you'll no longer be captive to the illusion of self-importance. You've been conditioned by culture and education to think of western spirituality as moving from Middle East to the west. This is false. It did move from east to west but in much smaller veins from its movement from west (Hibernia) to east, the land of Egypt. Most of your western religious structure is the foundation of Egypt but let it be known Egypt resides as a solar cult whose higher mind arose from its gnosis which came from two main sources, Hibernia which is now called Ireland and the Dogon, which is now Sudan.

So few will research the epistemology of the Scythians, Celts, and Gauls to see the words and trails of linguistics as they were actually laid down. One of the most obvious is the famous pillars of Hercules of the Greeks. These pillars are none other than the pillars of Ogman of the hexagonal stones of giant's causeway in Northern Ireland, and the same features appear off eastern Scotland. Seafarers of old traverse continuously from Egypt to the isles of Britain not only for trade but more so to be initiated into the great schools of the druidic astronomers. The druids gave rise to sacred knowledge of the tree people known as the yew people. This is where the word Jew comes from. Jewish is not a race or ethnicity, it is a certain people of initiation into sacred knowledge of the yew tree. Most depictions of great masters are sitting with or under a tree symbol; this is the yew tree in most cultures. Buddha, Krishna, Yeshua, Jesus, Odin, Moses and the burning bush and so on. The tree is an ancient symbol of knowledge.

There is a deep seated tie of knowledge between the Irish (rishis/sages) and the Egyptian (gypt-sies) which tell a story of earth history only half told. Know for sure that half the story has NEVER been told, and when it is, you humans will stand in the light. These are but twigs in the tree of truth. The whole truth in its reality holds a vibration of intensity that man has not prepared himself for, he must raise his vibration out of materialism in order for his consciousness to tune or grasp it. Conquer and conquest will never deliver one's soul to the truth.

Also, the Levites come from the druidic word for the rowan tree called Lewi. The Lewi tree became the people of the lewi tree. Over time called Luis, and Levite. The druidic colleges at old times were all over the world from India to

Northern Africa to Ireland. The land of Ireland was called Hibernia. Also it was written as Hiber, In Egypt (eber) and then Hebrew which meant one who was initiated into higher knowledge. Again they are not a race but more of a caste of people.

And in Egypt, much later, the Israelites fled as they were thrown out by the corrupted families of certain pharaohs who still fill their hearts with avarice today. The pharaohs became ego bound with the Hyksos peoples also called the shepherd kings. This culture corrupted the kingship by teaching the love of money and the so called power of it. The ruler/pharaoh named Akhenaten divided himself from the amenists when he became the most oppressive ruler by serving only himself and his own family. He brought in the concept of monotheism to the natural theology of the solar worshiper but did so only under his own family's personal aspect of the sun. Which is ultimately separatism. He later became the head of the atonists which derived from the name Akhen aton. Atonists from his line are and worship the god Seth or set which is a sinister aspect of solar light. They exploit and enslave but have never learned to ascend back light through consciousness. They believe themselves above others and call it loyalty and enjoy the pain of others as entertainment.

As such this line of perpetual plunder still shows itself today as the modern version of the Hyksos with their symbols, the red cross, red shield, double cross, and double horseman, key and crown, and others. They mock the sacred symbols in order to pervert them. They mock the pyramid, the serpent, the obelisk, the lion, the eye, the swastika, the cross in order to confuse the sacred and original meaning of symbols. They also mock holy lands, places, and temples with corrupt education and dispensation of lies and advertising. They franchise temples into a business of churches. Now through the age of Pisces they have so corrupted the solar consciousness of Horus/Christ by editing the scriptures and deifying the solar sun as a literal man. Worshipping a literal man causes the loss of attunement with the solar power that runs through all men, the planet, and sustenance. While splintering the psyche of man by offering the fragment that some men may be created unequal to others." Thot then said with a rasp "bowing before the unknown is nearly pointless, but bowing at the feet of a man is foolish absurdity."

He paused, I had no questions. He spoke in such a way that I felt his words to be authentic, so I just did my best to digest. He said further, that a great example of this perversion of meaning these thieves dispense is the connotation of the word Aryan. Most westerners think it is a negative and racist meaning, this is not so. The root is Ari, and engraved on the walls of Denderah in Egypt, in the time of king Pepi. It was written by the people who drew the plans for building the great pyramid. They were followers of Horus (sun god) and were called the Nu-er-nub-ari. Which means the keeper of secrets, namely the secrets of how to build such a structure with such precision. This is from the Ari of the druids and their relations with Egypt. The druidic Ari (also Eri) were teachers and called the keepers of truth. Since the druids were originally from the north (Hibernia), Aryans became known as people from the north. Its roots refer to erin, Ireland, aries, to arise, eric, erect, to stand in truth.

Even this is written six thousand year ago in Sanskrit texts referring to Aryans. The connection between these regions is very old indeed. We see it yet again in the naming of the city of London which is rightly Elludon then Elondon in reference to El or Elohim meaning messengers of God. The Elohim are the seven visible planets who reflect the sun's light in moving ways to message man in his psycho-spiritual body. This city was before this named Llud (Lugh), the Irish sun god and was the temple of the sun. And the people's pope calls himself the vicar of Christ or viceroy, which literally means stand in for Christ. He is blatantly telling the world that he is creating a vicarious relationship between the worshiper and Christ, giving himself the power to judge, rule, and condemn as long as followers acquiesce. These families of ancient corruption divided the kingdoms of all lands in order to polarize and conquer, it's one of the oldest tricks in the book (the book of man), it's written in the book. You must learn by keen discernment to read the words, and tones and this is only done by accessing the right side of the brain.

The following are more roots of the common syllables of Israel (Is-Ra-El), which refer to Egyptian gods Isis, Ra, Elohim. Meditate on these and feel their vibration. Here are some Ra (words) —Ra'ah (Shepard)

-Rais (means president)

-Rabbi (teacher of the torah)

-radio (ray of dios, god)

-radius (ray of dios, source)

-pharaoh (pa or father-ra)

-pyramid (mid fire)

-ram (ra)

-Ramses (ra ma or father-mother)

-brahma (solar higher mind)

-chakra (chi, cha, ka or energy of ra the sun)

-quran   (ka-soul of ra)

- IS RA EL- (divine connotation in scientifically created languages, isis ra and elohim)

-Abraham (father ra)

-scarab sacra (sacral, sacred)

Thot went on to dissect the root tones of many words in the western world and brought out many corresponding meanings to them.   He reminded me that like language itself, not all rules apply at all times, there needs to be the development of syntax and context recognition when using this skillset of finding true meaning in ancient root words. He also told me that many scientifically made languages trace their origin to the fractal and wave formations made by the sun as it passes through the sky in a day.

Thot began to shift gears when he asked me of my understanding of history. "You see," he said, "history is of course HIS -STORY and mystery (MY-STORY), is of course your story. The mystery is your perspective or vantage of your own history. More importantly it is how truthful you are in telling it back to yourself. To be true you must be vigil and conscious but leave your self-importance out of it. Let's talk about Egypt.

The land of Giza is the land of Osiris and his son is Horus and their story is so similarly the same as your modern Christ. You have to ask yourself why? Horus is divinely conceived, resurrected, and known as the morning star. His mother Isis collected and put Osiris back together after he was opposed and chopped into 14 pieces by Set. Set is Osiris's brother and is the same personality as Cain, Thomas, or the opposer satan. The opposer is the prideful ego, the one who disconnects from his own inner light. Egyptians seek to be with the father Osiris when they die, so they live a life leading them toward the stars of Orion where he dwells. This is the same as christians seeking heaven when they die. In order to do so, they are judged, as so Tehuti/Thoth weighs the heart of Egyptians at death to judge their worthiness to pass through the gates. Tehuti writes the sacred hieroglyphs for them so as to impart the language of the heavens to the judged.

If man is intimately connected to the heavens and promised a place there upon death, he must learn the language of the heavens to display his concepts and harmony with the natural order. This sacred tongue is the spark of expansion, the way we speak within to the spirit. All truth lies within. To expand the spark, the initiate leaps through death to uncover what lies beneath the personal mask to reveal the true self.

Christian politics have stolen the most sacred philosophies from Egypt and plagiarized them as their own, all along losing and contorting their sacred and original meaning. The images of Mary holding the infant Jesus is the ancient Isis holding Horus and as you follow through the cult of Mithraism and Dionysus and others you can easily track the stolen psychology. The announcement of Baby Horus is thus the same. This announcement is the appearance of the star Sirius, some 2,000 years ago on December the 25th just after sunset, the Orion constellation appears and calls in the rising of Sirius just after. As then and now still this is called the salvation of Horus/Jesus.

The 3 stars of the belt of Orion are what is called the 3 magi who announced the star of the east, which marks the event. It becomes blasphemous that modern humans don't know these obvious truths in history, and the lack of connection to the truth further fragments them. Humans need only sit under a beautiful tree and be still to realize his psyche adjusts to the nature around him, because it is made of that nature. He must tune himself to become the natural harmonic, or else he remains fearful and fragmented in his psyche."

I asked Thot, "how does one come to know the true history of such things?"

He said, "the answer to that is embedded in the mystery and must be tapped with one's intuitions combined with syncing multiple sciences, research, and philosophies together and is daunting but absolutely worth the endeavor. There is more, so much more, have you any memory or knowledge of Orkney?"

I said only that I knew it was off the great Scottish coast.

Thot then said, "this is now your investigation to pursue, dig into and practice syncing the messages of history and use your intuition to discover their true history."

I agreed to study the history of Orkney. He went on.

He said, "If you speak of your discoveries be prepared for ridicule as most people are terrified of the truth. The average mind is trained to be feeble and rigid and it's aptitude for understanding knowledge is infantile. Tell people what I am about to tell you about reality, and you will soon find friendships dissolve, but this does not mean the truth is not true. Here, chew on this. The human body is the tree of life and the temple of God. As above so below. Hermetic principles went underground during battles and wars of kings and Pharaohs. The Hyksos pharaohs or shepherd kings, controlled the church through magic, money, and media and are the fish people of today. They enslaved consciousness in a box so that people will not realize they are the temple of God or that consciousness, by design, is specular and completely fluid and renewing each moment. The only way to realize this is by process of initiating, self-induced initiation. The teaching of this knowledge has been suppressed, systematically, by the royal elite political hierarchy. So Hinduism, Buddhism, Taoism, Toltec, Lakota, Native American, aboriginal, certain tribes, the druids, all teach self-realization, self-initiation, or personal enlightenment. And this is what we have to go back to. Syncretism is a way of syncing and linking your thought process and perception to the harmony, fluidity and renewal of every moment. So truly, half the story of history has never been told.

Angelic, higher consciousness or beings of light are not alien, they are intrinsic energetic bundles of consciousness, either on their way to immortality or have already attained it. They seed man's consciousness at specific opportunistic times in which man can be lead in natural ways of procuring his enlightenment. Even the spirits of natural elements; certain plants, such as psilocybin mushrooms, ayahuasca or other sacred plants talking to shamans, are all door opening processes of initiation. Man has not stumbled upon them, he has been lead to them by higher consciousness.

4

Wheel in the Sky

hot and I found our way to a small stone house at the base of a small pine mountain. The tall trees sprung up behind the dwelling which is made of grey stones, I assume the stones are some sort of granite. Some of the stones are reddish and smooth, as if polished somehow. His house was dim even in midday, but extremely comfortable and inviting. Soon a fire pops on the hearth and smells of peat. The rich smell sends me into a state of memory. I am in a place where I am not immediately recalling anything clear but slightly on the verge of recalling something important. This state just continues perpetually, so I find myself daydreaming or entranced all the time. He speaks and I talk back and we converse but I drift off in a rhythmic pattern and try to refocus. This happens over and over, it sort of confuses me but somehow I don't mind.

He prompts me and asks, "why did you find me?"

I replied, "I thought you found me on the path outside

the cave."

He said, "I was minding my mental duties and you arrived within my standing place on the path, so you found me."

I didn't care, so I ask "why do you care who found who, does it matter?"

"Matter," he said, "indeed it does hold matter. Your intention is how you found me and your intention is the driving of matter itself."

"How so?"

"You are human and so it goes in all the ages, light and dark, that you humans by design are manifesters of matter, the material world."

"What on earth are do you mean," I asked?

"Just open your eyes, listen intently and you'll see. "He spoke, for what seemed a long time and confusion and daydreams came over me, I listened and processed.

"You see," he said, "humans are intrinsically created to co-create reality here on the planet with their thinking prowess. What you hold in your mind and articulate in vision tends to manifest in the reality you behold. Look here, see this sword and this harp, how did they appear here? Humans have ideas, which become obsessive thoughts and soon after, a sword is here and this harp too. Do you think God in the heavens created this harp? No, God created all organic and inorganic elements that make up the harp. He created the consciousness to think and dream it up, but you humans created it and play it for him. Humans created letters and writing, and the names of things as too describe the universe but the descriptions are not the objects themselves, they are mere descriptions. Still, the inner voice inside your mind is incessantly talking and this is a never ending description of the reality you sense. The deeper your awareness of what you sense, the deeper your reality is.

The trouble comes when you pin down reality in a description and then think that's where it ends. Here you focus attention on your world and so miss the rest of the world around you. In order to create reality, you have to tap into its flow and flux. It's like stepping into a river that moves in new ways around your body as you enter. The flow is relating to you as your body changes the waves filling in around you and your movements. These have never occurred this way before, and will never again. The moment of your relationship to the flow is present in this moment. If you look away, you cease to increase your awareness of the flow and thus repeat a looping pattern of what you once witnessed.

Co- creating your reality is using what you were aware of a moment ago to build what you see now in this moment. Your thoughts uphold the reality you see and manifest by your internal voice repeating itself over and over again. If I hit you with the scabbard of this sword and repeat the painful words (you hit me, you hit me, you hit me) over and over again then, the pain of those words will echo enough times to seep into your subconscious mind. There it will feed itself back to your conscious mind again and you will be in pain forever. The same occurs with the heartfelt thoughts and vibrations of love. The problem with humans is very few know they co-create reality or take responsibility for it when they do. Often vice over takes them through the senses. It's important to hear the words of Saint Agustin, 'A man has as many masters as he has vices.'

When vice rules the thoughts and the inner voice, people are living in the lower chakras or energy centers of the body. When they focus on loving all they encounter then the energy of the heart becomes activated as a bridge for the higher center and the living mind is forever altered. The higher mind can attain such virtues that it can offer a co-creation never before created to the spirit and heave up the opportunity for it to be accepted by the light of consciousness itself. The heart is the bridge of the chakras, the energy centers of the human body. This basic principle has been spoken of by many ascended masters or sons of the sun throughout your earth history. Mithras said it, Herne said it, Horus of Egypt said it, Mazda said it, Yeshua (Jesus) said it: 'thou shalt not reach the father except through me'. They all bring the message of reaching the highest consciousness chakra by bridging the low chakras through the loving heart to the higher chakras. Little king bear, if you can concentrate and listen I will show you how to turn vice into virtue. I will show you the power of the inner voice, the potent power of words."

He nudged me on my left shoulder and I snapped back to a waking state. I had not heard a word he said, for some time. I realized I had fallen asleep but it must have just been a few minutes. He stared at me intently with no facial expression, the only features not statuesque were his eyes, they were calibrating while he stared. I apologized, he said nothing. I asked him to continue and he lit and smoked a long stem pipe that smelled savory, deep and pleasant. I wondered what I was smelling and felt it was otherworldly and still magnificent. His pipe had two small snakes carved upon it and at the bowl , carved was a small set of feathered wings. It was perfectly crafted. I wanted to ask him if I could smoke but felt to awkward to do so. Just then he spoke.

He pointed the stem at me as if he meant business; he had one eye closed and the other peering at me sideways. "This is not for you to partake, this pipe looks like wood and ceramic from earth but it is not. It is made of mercury and forged there within, you only see it in familiar terms to your earthly eyes, and this is the way of all vibratory communication. If you have eyes to see alternate vibrations or ears to hear, they will be added unto you. I speak to you in your native tongue like you would speak to a baby in his. Your awareness is your only filter and if you see or hear only with the intellect then you only see the world of the material. If you see or hear the awareness of God, then you see well beyond the confines of the material. Your body is a material filter but your energy centers will change the vibratory frequency of your body to a more receptive vessel. There is so much light beyond the spectrum you currently know. Your body has the potential to attune to the vibration of the spirit world, if you choose to do so.

He continued. Those you call ancients knew this. The human race is much older than you know, so your idea of ancient is very young to me. The people of Egypt, Mesoamerica, Sumer, Greece, and Africa and India knew this sacred knowledge. They knew it, because they were taught in mystery schools of synchronicity. Each initiate would go through a series of levels that usually took forty years to complete. The education they received was the holistic view of all of nature and its cycles of creation, destruction, and renewal. For thousands of years, people lived in truth and

47

knowledge of the science of light. Like a plant rooted beneath the ground, they know exactly who, what, why, how, and where the sun is. They knew the source that bestowed and powered their life and death. I'll explain but you must open your ears to listen."

As he said that, an echo and vibration of his last word (listen) slowly repeated and faded into silence.

He said, "The ancients knew that the seven visible planets correspond to the chakra energy centers in the body. They knew that each change of the planets, affected the energy of themselves, so in turn they kept close watch on the heavens and the changes. This way they recorded the changes that occurred and so created a guide book of how to reach the heavens through ascending each chakra and each planet. They attain higher and higher states of awareness and vibration."

I asked, "why are there seven visible planets and thus seven chakras?" I was not sure I agreed with him, although he spoke with some tone of definitiveness, I still questioned him.

He said, "simple, seven is a sacred number, a builder of the creation of light and the universe at large. Seven attunes to man and anatomically builds his vibratory structure in reference to infinity. Poor man, has forgotten his own divine nature. Seven encodes infinity."

"How so," I asked?

"Seven and its letters hold a pattern for numbers, so each letter in the alphabet has a number value assigned to it. Hebrew, Greek, and other languages were designed the same way. In English, which is the language of angles (of light), the letter A equals one, B equals 2 and so on in sequences up to M. It starts over at N equaling 1, O equaling 2 and so on. In this way you add the numbers of the letter of seven and this equals 22. Now divide 22 by 7 and it equals Pi (3.14), one of the transcendental numbers that never ends. It is infinite! The ratio of Phi (1.618) is the other infinitely coded number. As man perceives his universe he can see seven colors in the light spectrum, the rainbow (rainbow is referring to arc or bow of Ra=sun god). He hears seven notes in an octave (the last is the first); he has seven chakras; he is thus governed by seven planets, and thus built his week upon seven days. Each day refers to the influence of one celestial body, so Sunday is the sun, Monday is the moon, Tuesday is Mars, Wednesday is Mercury, Thursday is Venus, Friday is Jupiter, and obviously Saturday is Saturn. In this way, man sees the world around him through his own design, he see his own infinite nature all around and through himself.

Now listen. The sky you see today has changes upon changes, deeply encoded in itself. To see the sky and its celestial bodies raises your consciousness and tunes it to the emanations of the solar system in this moment. The planets and their movements bring forth an elasticity to the awareness of the people in the system. An elasticity to each day. It has always done this and what you need to understand is that the sky of the ancients looked quite different than what you see and feel today. Many thousands of years ago, the planet Saturn came close to Earth in its helical trajectory. This caused a multitude of shifts on Earth, and to its creatures and consciousness. Saturn was so close that it appeared bigger than the sun, so it dominated the sky. This went on for a few thousand years and eventually it's electric force due to proximity caused destruction and calamity on earth. But before the calamity a golden age began with the Saturnian, the creation of your myths and archetypes dawned in this age.

Its name was called many different things and Saturn was given to it in roman times, also the original name of the city, of Rome itself. And before that it was called Atum and was overpowering the sun. At times it was called El, and Kronos, and Bale, and its reign was of beauty and abundance. The orb changed the sky not only visibly but its solar light, vibration, magnetism, and electricity bent the consciousness of man upward (spiraling) toward an age of enlightenment. The visual symbol of this you can still see today on stone art, statues, reliefs and drawing of gods and wise men holding a wheel or sitting on the throne of a wheel. The wheel is a timepiece but not like a wristwatch, it marks the golden age and its ruthless descent to the dark age."

"Why the wheel," I asked?

"The wheel is what people of Earth saw for thousands of years in the sky. The alignment of Saturn, Venus and Mars drew a bulls eye in the sky, so a sphere inside a sphere inside a smaller sphere. The red Mars was closest and Venus in between. The plasma discharge of electromagnetic light from Saturn bent itself as spokes of a wheel around Venus and then Mars appeared as the center or hub. It was a magnificent sight to see and people recorded in stone all over the globe, each with a slightly different viewpoint. This vision morphed and changed over time into many different plasma wheel-like shapes and thus gave rise to multiple archetypes gods in the sky. Most notable is the depiction of Venus as a women standing in a sea shell. The rays of plasma resemble the upward diagonals of a shell and personified in human female form is the beautiful lady of Venus you see in European frescos today.

This great conjunction of spheres appeared as a radiant eight spoked wheel or disc of light with a red center. And over time a luminous crescent of light began at the bottom, this was shining from the sun upon Saturn. The crescent then moved to the side offering different configurations. It was named the wheel of Babylon, the shamash and star of Ishtar. The Venus aspect of the configuration was named the mother, the feminine. The red Mars was named the warrior. Each movement of these three gave rise to new figures in the minds of men. The red Mars began to drop so its light bent downward looked like a red tongue and you see this in the tongue of medusa, and the warrior god of the center of the mayan calendar (Tlaltecuhtli). As the bodies disassembled the light of Venus became steamy and disorganized giving her a frightening appearance.

The configuration was truly incredible in its variety as due to the electrical nature of plasma discharge. The number of spokes, arms, or streamers took on all kinds of imagery based on the helical nature and intensity of the discharge. As planets approach each other they exchange electric discharge and electric columns are formed in all kinds of shapes. The thunderbolt of Zeus is one of these shapes, he wields the bolt of electric power as a god. It also morphed into the famous bull of heaven. As time went on we saw plasma discharges in many shapes and one is still common among myths today. The thunderbolt of Thor and Zeus, these were pronged fork-like columns of light in the sky. The Gods have been depicted throughout the Mediterranean for thousands of years now with this very odd shaped bolt. Did you ever think to wonder how it got the shaped and design we see today? At some point it moved into oblivion, the entire configuration. The bodies drifted away from view and continued along their specific and unique orbits. Eventually every planet and star dies and when they do, they spin their faces of radiation slower and in more erratic patterns. The slower they spin the more you can become aware of the light legs. Light legs are just like the legs of a spider. The spider is a brilliant little star itself, a very accurate reflection of a star. When a spider is in full force and you see its little legs running from you, you miss the legs, they move so fast they become radiant like the pulsing light of a star. Energy is rapidly being thrown off the body of that little spider like the wings of a bee. But the next time you're feeling sinister, thump a spider in the brain just hard enough to watch it die slowly."

I felt this was a bit morbid, and I could tell that so did he. He was illustrating a point. He continued. "You'll see the odd, erratic, wave like movements of the legs of that little arachnid. They move at random times and twitch like a worm under water. Then one by one, they cease. Then the last leg rotates, and wriggles, and you see that leg cresting like a sine wave, up and down and around, like a whip. Then stillness! Those legs are the pulses and waves of light electrically flapping in the dark light of space, as the star spins its last spin and arcs its last spiral. Resting finally as a shell of being: simple dust in the universe. Many astrologers see these erratic star movements as a binary system with another star. This binary wobble has never been confirmed.

Sirius (the star) may be cause for procession of the equinoxes but it may simply be the wobble of the entire Solar System that reveals these movements. The binary system could express two stars being burst out of the galactic core as they unwind outwards from their birthplace (the core). The binaries wrap around each other grouping as a whole, their trajectories are helical in nature as they spiral further and further away from their birthplace. The procession of the equinoxes could simply be the entire galaxy undulating and wobbling its (arachnid) arms in electric wave patterns, as this is an obvious symptom of the electric universe we live in. The idea of gravity is irrelevant here because, electric current does not move in a straight line, like all other movements in manifestation it moves in spirals. What most think is gravity is really spiralling electrical vortices seeking rest or equipotential in other spiraling electrical vortices of complimentary pressure conditions. In essence gravity does not exist. What does though is shafts of still magnetic light, we call vortices, which center space geometries by constantly seeking rest or equilibrium. In order for you to grasp this, you must unlearn what you think you know.

I am teaching you this sacred science because you have found me in your dream, in the nagual, The infinite part of yourself. As I said before you humans have lost your way, and forgotten who you are and your purpose here. The light of all creation is calling the Earth beings at this time. The time of the galactic alignment is beginning, it is in your holy books but you know not the language to read it, even though you see the words on the page. All communication is movement, it is of a vibratory nature and is encased in its own unique syntax. You have to understand the syntax to decode the message embedded in the words. Your time has been the last 2,100 years of the age of the fish (pisces), it has been ruled by the planet Jupiter. In so, much transgression, greed, and corruption has been brought forth by the business of the church. So much, so that very few can read the message in the holy books.

Still, like in all times, the messages that man receives world-wide and simultaneously are always written in the night's sky. So it is upon us now as it has been written by the anointed consciousness of many thousands of cycles ago, that when the sign of man appears on the horizon of the equator in the east, the ascension is near. This sign is staring you in the face, and the harvesting of souls to higher vibratory bands is occurring for the next 2,100 years. The age of the franchises of churches is dissolving. The Saturnians are found out and will have to give up the game they've been cheating in. If man knew from which he was molded, this process would be as natural as the changing of the seasons. I will always remind you, first and foremost your wisest duty is to yourself. Know thyself!

The return to soul and self-divinity is blossoming now in the sign of man, it's the only sign of the twelve that is a man (the water bearer) aquarius. Vibration is the source of all phenomena and here on earth, your strongest source is the most obvious, look up and behold the sun. It powers all vibration in your system, without it none of your consciousness would survive to peer through your senses. The rock would be frozen and colder than hell. The sun electrically impregnates the planets, and they absorb and reflect this electric light in divine geometries and angles. The angles (angels) carry forth the growth of consciousness from light to flesh. From light to flesh is a process of building angles so as to become more dense, until on earth these angles vibrate as matter (solid). The aspects of the planets affect the physical, psychic, and spirit of man through the law of correspondence. Man's body corresponds to the solar bodies and the universe at large. Know thyself."

"How do we men remember this heritage, and how did

we forget so easily," I asked? Thot said, "it's simple, you went to sleep and haven't woken yet. You only dreamt that you awoke. The nagual, you enter, because you know somewhere deep within that you are capable of the awareness of total freedom. Total freedom is union with infinity. This is the beginning of waking up. Open up your heart and mind, abracadabra! You don't realize the planets effects on you? Of course you do. The sun hits your body and you feel it warming, or burning your skin. You run from the coolness of the shade tree and bath in the light of the golden king. Do you not also feel the lovely moon pulling the tides within you? The moon pulls the oceans all along the shores in a rhythm and she pulls the unfertilized egg from woman down and out of her body. Are you so stuck in the left brain that you can't feel her? I say, all the seven visible planets weigh in in their own ways upon the body, mind, and soul of you. You only have to listen in stillness to see it is so. The larger ones are gas giants, and so are composed of an ethereal vibration, and they therefore affect you in a more ethereal way, their light angles are the geometries of ether. Some plants are watery and some are fiery, and some are solid and dense. Each vibration resends its signature light angles within you in respecting ways. These bodies in the macrocosm are the same bodies inside your body, the microcosm."

Pondering the concept/natural and mystical law (as above so below), I find myself awake again in a new day. I realize I am not with Thot and not in the mountain pines. I am going about my daily business and I am in the light of day, thinking about the words of Thot. Thinking about his view of knowledge, perception and universal mind and vast awareness. Thinking. I begin to do my research; I find the lectures of Maurice Cotterell, and most notably his discoveries of sunspot cycles. He starts again by speaking of specific seals, symbols, and glyphs that encode sacred Maya, Aztec, and Toltec knowledge.

"The Maya knew the correct number for the cycle of

sunspots, they knew its effect on us and recorded it in important ways. In 3113 BCE, they started their calendar. This starting point is not arbitrary, it marks the last time the magnetic reversal of the sun's poles occurred. The planet Venus had a pole reversal as well, but the Earth did not because it is further away from the sun. They called it the birth of Venus and now Venus is rotating upside down and slowed its rotation. This is called a sunspot mini moon, and it causes a mini ice age. When we have a mini ice age, less evaporation of the oceans occurs and this change in the sun's radiation waves effects melatonin in the body chemistry of man. Melatonin has a direct effect on fertility and thus spontaneous fetal abortion. During the sunspot mini moon, the earth's population decreases due to harsh conditions and less fertility across the globe.

The sun emits four patterns of radiation each month, so one each week. There is a rhythm to the timing while the sun rotates; its poles and equator rotating at different rates. One side or imitation is unseen each week, so it is there but on the side facing away from earth, so its effect is absent until it comes around again. The rhythm is showering down on fertile embryos and causes a timing to be synchronized in the new life. The DNA is literally charged with life giving sunlight. After all, the word chromosomes means color or spectrum of light, which is what we are, light beings. We are powered by the sun and its light, refracted through the planets. Cells divide, grow, and divide further and the hormones begin to sync with the sun, this is why the pineal gland is light responsive and light sensitive and has piezoluminescence cells. This is why melatonin responds back to the sun for fertility timing. As we grow, our king gland regulates the rhythmic radiation of the sun cycle with the cell growth of the body. If they are in sync, the body will be healthy and grow but if carcinogens are introduced via damage, food, or stress the syncing of the cycle becomes off and cancer or degeneration of the cells occurs. The body, will die unless corrected.

We also know that sunshine causes influenza and other viruses or illnesses to mutate. This is what is known as a sun blister or fever blister. We can cure many illness once we understand the pattern of the sides of the sun on individuals. The pattern is set in utero so there are four main sides or patterns to the sun and so four main types of patterns in the DNA of people. The four faces of the sun as it rotates on its axis sends out radiating patterns unique to each face. The timing of these patterns infuses and encodes DNA and marks an imprint relative to the sun's location and light in that moment.

The sun affects our four bodies as well. We all have a physical, mental, emotional, and spiritual body. The sun has forever been worshiped as God because all our religious figures and stories are but personifications of the sun and the solar system. All lasting spiritual texts affirm that God is light and that he created man in his own image, thus it is clearly stated that man is in fact light. We are divine light rays (emanations) of the sun condensed through atomic sacred geometric forms into the density of physical bodies. We depend on the sun for all of life because we are the sun in a dense vibratory form. This is why our consciousness can be the lamp of enlightenment. In the physical world all creatures must replicate themselves in order to grow. We must generate and sacrifice a part of ourselves (the seed) to grow a new life. This is the true sacrifice given to God and this is what God has given of himself to create us.

Energy is equal to matter times the speed of light squared; which describes the physical world in opposite polarity of the spirit or God. As we ascend the path process to light we increase our energy and its wave frequency. The frequency of God is the wave form infinite. God is not only light but also love. If we learn to love ourselves completely we attain higher soul vibration or voltage, this expands our material consciousness into the awareness of infinite consciousness. Infinite consciousness we can love all, and others completely. We thus become unconditioned still light. This entire process is not only our growth of human soul voltage but the growth of the universe expanse or God itself. If you hate yourself or the world or others, you never increase your soul voltage and you remain bound by matter and gravity and remain in hell. The heart is truly where love happens, and love is the guide vibration to God. The ascended masters, avatars of christus consciousness are the light of love. They are plucked by the natural causes of enlightenment like the wind blows seeds of the daisy flower.

The Mayans knew this. Wow, how clever they were. Their attunement came to them by seeking, paying attention, and study. They know the sun's ecliptic is responsible for the earth, air, water, and fire signs of the people. They know the angles of the sun's rays control and power life on this planet. They know the zodiac (mazzaroth) is the mathematical map of the heavens and the languages of consciousness. This point is illustrated by countless encoded scriptures. The thing is, none of spiritual scripture is written to be literal; the depth of message is in parable or allegory. And further still, there are root words and math gematria that shines light deeper still to the true meaning meant by scriptures such as the bible.

The initiated and high priests of antiquity knew the languages and how to decode it, but they purposefully withheld this knowledge from the public. Some abused its power while others dispensed it to those who were genuinely seeking the true knowledge of self. This knowledge is now no longer just the wheel in the sky, it is now here for those who seek it with the true heart and will keep it held in the sacred chamber.

A brief example in the Bible, when Jesus (Yeshua, IHS) observed the apostles from the shore, they were fishing. He asked if they had caught any fish, they said no. He suggested to throw the net on the right side of the boat (which represents the right side or intuitive side of the brain), and behold they caught fish. They caught exactly 153 fish, and why? The number is not arbitrary, as none in the book are. The 153 fish is referring, in coded fashion, to the sacred symbol called the vesica pisces. This symbol is the way cells divide themselves to generate and birth new life. A cell or circle known as Pi (3.14), when divided evenly, creates an almond or eye shape. The shape mathematically has a ratio of 153 from nucleus to nucleus, and the story is referring to the sacred geometric shape the vesica pisces or vessel of Pi, which is the womb of creation on the cellular and atomic level. Furthermore, once you know the 153 ratio, with this line you can also now measure the height of the vesica pisces which works out to be 265. This ratio is present in all of nature and when you divide 265 by 153 it equals the square root of 3. The 3 is referring back to the holy trinity (Shiva,

Brahma, Vishnu) of transcendental creation which is 3.14; rooted in the vessel of creation. The meaning of the word itself Pisces tells us what it means. Pi is referring to the never ending circle and scis means to split or cut, this is where we get the word scissors, we cut with them. So it is literally the splitting of Pi and this is how all of creation is birthed. The story has nothing to do with fish, it has to with using the higher mind of the right brain (intuition) to acquire knowledge. And of course Jesus is the symbol of the fish, because he rules the sign of pisces for the last 2,160 years, which is one procession sign of the zodiac.

It is no coincidence that in English gematria, which is the numerical encoding of the alphabet, the words Jesus Christ encode the number 2,160. Horus, and Yeshua also add or multiply to exactly 2,160, which is again the number of years in one processional sign of the zodiac. This is telling us that Jesus and Horus are the same archetype for the solar body we call the sun, and yes they were both the son of God. The letters Jesus Christ also encode the exact radius (432,000 miles) and diameter (864,000 miles) of the sun. The mathematical probability of this being luck, chance, or coincidence is astronomical. The stars and the solar system not only give birth to us and life on earth, they give birth to all our theology. The wheel in the sky is sometimes clearly visible and speaks to us directly, while other times, it is so vast, we are unaware that we are even looking at it.

Remember also, that the great pyramid serves as an (male\female procreation) it was built to reveal Pi (3.14), the circle. The number 40 in mythical terms is always symbolic of the wise or initiated. This number 40 is always storied; like 40 days in the wilderness, or 40 years wandering in exile, or 40 days and nights. These are clearly not literal occurrences for the wise ones, it is a symbolic meaning, that those who knew the significance of 40 were initiated into the meanings encoded into the pyramid. 22 x 40 = 880, 7 x 40 = 280, pyramid ratio = 880:280. The base of the Great Pyramid is then multiplied by 2 (2 Pi x r), 2 x 880 = 1,760. So the number 40 is known to encode the base of the pyramid (1,760), it's height (280 cubits), the square base represented as a circle, and the unit of measure itself (the Egyptian cubit). This number 1,760 is still the number of yards in the imperial mile. The significance of this number on a larger scale is important because this measure is a true measure of the nature of the earth size and sphere itself. The pyramid was built to hold and reveal many truths to man about man and the natural order of his earth body as well as his celestial one.

If you're asking why this is important, the dots are still disconnected for you, initiation has not yet begun. The structure resonates knowledge to the eyes open to see it. Tracking precession cycles, solstices, and equinoxes are but the beginning of its lessons. This sacred knowledge reveals a way that humans maintain harmony with life by attuning to nature. It is both an observatory of earth measures and celestial ones that teach us physically we can reach infinity. It has the potential power to teach the self-awareness of immortality. Why is this important for mankind? Because man must never be lead so far astray to forget how to procreate light and consciously take responsibility for creating and imprinting the qualities of his own soul."

Thot switched his thinking and took a deep breath. It was noticeable that his mind was drawing on some knowledge coming into him at this instant, it was as if I could witness something from outer space communicating directly to him, causing him to shudder, and shift gears. His eyes shimmered like moonlight, they danced. He began to talk in a different way, a new cadence. He said, "this will further build on your understanding of the wheel in the sky, although you may not fully grasp its meaning until later. Just follow and track with me. There is a key point you should know called Atum, the name given to God in predynastic Egypt, this is before foreigners invaded and took over the sacred city of Heliopolis. Atum is both the name of God and the symbol of the earth, it is the solar cross, this is how Christianity is linked to ancient Egypt and her medicine. This symbol became the symbol of the atom so the name etymologically carries its meaning, Atum is atom and is the science to prove or reveal the way that light moves through the universe. It is two ways of saying the same thing.

All the planets are spit out of the equator of stars or suns. In this process our solar system was born and our planets move in a vortex in the wake of our sun. As the planets move further away from the Sun they expand in size, so our earth is expanding at this time and the axial rotation speeds up in order to balance the centrifugal and centripetal forces in order to keep the planets within the vortex of its father sun. As their rotation speeds up the planet's orbit slows down. This is the basic balance of the way light manifesting material bodies moves throughout the universe and this symbol can be seen mathematically and geometrically as solstices and equinoxes which in essence is the solar cross.

This vortex, created by star/sun, moves through space in a spiraling motion. In the same way the word spirit refers to eternal creation or motion, the spirit is the spiral. As all bodies in space move in curves or arcs, they form eternal spirals even when in orbit. Within the symbol of the solar cross you have balance; you have north, south, east, and west. The Medicine Wheel, the four directions, the balance of the universe. This symbol represents nature as it is light/dark, up/down, hot/cold, day/night, summer/winter, male/female, electric/magnetic and so on and so forth…yin and yang.

Why is this important? To all lovers of wisdom, or philosophers in life they seek improvement or progress within their being. Their progress always comes in thought, then speech, then action. The higher one's thought the higher one's speech and action in life. These are the teachings of the Hermetica.

The Hermetica is abstract or right brain thinking, this is actually unity consciousness or universal mind thinking or yoga. In order to use your right brain, you sync and link your intellectual opinions of the left brain into one holistic view. This is unity consciousness. Often people's personalities, opinions, and beliefs stand in their way from accessing their higher mind, higher consciousness, or unity thinking. You must learn to move outside of the intellect as the intellect was created and born of the abstract right brain quality.

We see this reflected to us in nature. When we look at nature we see subtle barriers of changing manifestations, but we see no end, it is infinite. We look to the cosmos and it goes on forever showing us that nature is in fact ordered intelligently as one unity with no end or boundary. For men to measure these things, he has to understand the concept of as above so below and as without so within. When he learns to see the universe as a large reflection of that which lies within himself, he realizes he is the microcosm of the macrocosmic universe. This is why the ancients drew the zodiac and Adam Kadmon (the human body in the stars), and the Kabbalah, and the chakra system, in the stars. They are mapping their own temple of God, which is the human body, in the cosmos simply because all the harmonics of the cosmos are enfolded by light within the human body. One is very small and one is very large but both are infinite and reflections of each other. Hermes is a personification of a cosmic principle, not unlike all sun gods or moon gods; like Jesus, Mithras, Zoroaster, Krishna, Osiris, Horus, Mithras, etc.

But we see here that Hermes is not one to be worshipped as he is a cosmic principle personified. Man gave him a personality in order so that he may never forget the principle of the cosmos that he embodies. Hermes is not one to be worshipped, he is the cosmic principle personified in order so that man may never forget the principle. Hermes is higher mind, higher consciousness, Christ consciousness, cosmic consciousness which cannot be reached through the lower mind, or the left brain of the human. The left brain is lower consciousness, the intellect chops up and compartmentalizes bits of your reality in order so that it may be processed one by one, in a linear fashion. It is only through higher mind that these small segments of reality are unified or synced together into wholeness, which is nature as a divine Being. Man, must have access to his higher mind or spirit in order to harmonize with the cosmos." Thot paused, and asked, "do you get it, do you understand? So many people don't, they choose to limit themselves to perceptions handed down to them by the blind, complacent, and fearful. So many choose to slumber. They in sleep, refuse to see that their own self is always intimately connected to nature and the subject/object relationship is an illusion. It is an illusion because as man communes with nature, so nature communes with man. Consciousness recognizes consciousness.

Truth is total freedom - the summit of all knowing. Without your body in its current form, you cannot contain and experience consciousness in the matter state. Without this form you cannot draw down the stars to you. You will in time, indeed, KNOW THY SELF! Truth is muddied and obscured by the illusion of mortality. Truth is the experience of reality without the existence of the self. When personality ceases, universality remains; cognition of total existence, freedom, infinity."

5

Viracochas and the Sunspots

he Viracochas of the Americas were masters of number and cycle. How they became such masters is only perceivable through speculation. Most scholars think, they simply sat, looked, and recorded everything of significance in the night sky for thousands of years. Over time, they became familiar with the trends, charted them, and attuned their conscious lives to these cycles. The thing to grasp here is that in order to understand the Viracochas, you must first understand number, at least in a general sense, then in an esoteric one. To begin to touch on numerical literacy I defer to the master philosopher of recent France R.A. Schwaller de Lubicz. He is most known for his brilliant decoding of the Egyptian temple of Man in Luxor. De Lubicz found layers of motivation, creativity, and meaning behind the Egyptian's purpose for constructing the massive architectural temples from the viewpoint of their eyes, revealing worlds of information into their psyche and spirit. Schwaller de Lubicz describes multi-dimensional consciousness required to understand numbers from a universal or astrological perspective:

"Consider for the moment the Greek philosophy in adopting the image of original being as, like width rather than like volume. This approach helped to deviate the primary paradigms of Western thought toward reductionist and mechanistic assumptions so that to plague modern man's relation to the natural world. All our thinking, designing, and engineering practices follow this model of using two - dimensional diagrams of points, lines, and planes, which are then superimposed on the physical world of Volume. But the reality of the natural world is exclusively three-dimensional, and, like a volume, inseparably binds opposed States; surfaces and interiors; front and back to mean: inside and outside to mean: top and bottom...We lack direct consciousness in space and time. We can only know them indirectly by means of mass, force, and energy, and by the intermediary of phenomena which may be tested by one or another of our five senses.

...Human beings then lack the two cents necessary for knowledge of all costs. From this imperfection, of which we are always being made aware, through this need everything is reduced to fundamental properties, without any attention ever being paid to the form of all the various effects of this universal organization. The result is that the science of numbers, the most wonderful guide to the continual creation of the universe, remains an enormous hypothesis. Its use has not awakened in the higher consciousness and by the deepest depth of knowledge, and we have not come to recognize numbers as truth nor experience the living relation with our own senses. To understand true succession in creation, one must know how the first, or abstract, nature of numbers develops, how multiplicity engages itself from unity. It is obvious that the first unity, without a Cause, is indivisible. There are not yet any seconds or, thirds, etc.

It is the first unity. Hence it is purely qualitative, without quantity. The first unity is always, although under different expressions, the idea of the absolute, of eternal, of the indefinite. This idea contains contraries, for example the same nature twice, but has posed in its tendencies, because the idea of an absolute can only exist as the perfect stabilization of the two essentially contrary natures. The stabilization cannot exist, since manifestation immediately follows from it. In the last analysis, it is this idea that is generally meant by the term cause without a cause. Nature possesses in itself, the tendency to make the definite out of the indefinite. The first one can therefore only create a multiplicity by qualitative addition, and never by multiplication, because multiplication is proper to procreation. It is in this way, then, that the number one gives 1 and 1 or and is by this fact, 3. The indivisible one creates or manifests the first divisible number, which is the number two. This number, in its abstract nature, is two and becomes one as a concrete indivisible unity. Such is the triple nature of the Creator and this creation is one, but a unified one manifested. According to the mystical explanation of numbers, the Creator God is referred to as this one, as Father, Son, and the spirit.

This is how numbers disengage from the abstract one— It has always been said that initiation occurs by and of itself. One cannot explain the life of things; one can only merge oneself with it as they feel it. In every epoch, therefore, the goal of all sacred initiatory institutions was to

give to whoever asked for it, the means of self-initiation—
Obviously, whoever knows the science perfectly will be able
to foresee many phenomena, and understand the necessity in
characteristic form of their evolution. In astrology numbers
possess a value unsuspected by the uninitiated. One must
not, however, attribute virtues other than those which there
are a reason to be. We shall begin by discerning that every
phenomenon comes to realization in three stages, as the
archaic symbolism of the circle, containing; circumference,
radius, and diameter teaches us wise things. We shall call
these three stages the cycles of polarization, ideation, and
formation respectively. With numbers, one can easily define
the time, movement, and force which separates and mediates
effect from its cause, but one must know (in the full sense of
the word), not the physical, but the occult or hidden costs.
This is humanly impossible, and only the super human being
has succeeded in merging with space, the only quality proper
to all things."

Yes discerning his meaning is both possible and
challenging, but rewarding. He is referring to the multiple
layers of dimensional meaning of the symbol, for in this case
we call, the number. The language of math and number is
abstract by design and so encodes incredible dimensionality.
If you are focused and deeply contemplative you may even
uncover the creativity inherent in all such abstract creations,
for in the abstract all potential exists, and we may mold this
potential into some fact (manifested idea), and this brings
into existence the lateral or non-abstract, that so many
people crave for security. They, locked in fear and intellect
alone, will not allow themselves to uncover their true
potential. In Luxor, we now know the temple of man is
constructed as a human body, but not just its physical form.
The stone blocks, measured with precise numbering,

creatively holds volume, depth, width as symbols of emotion, creativity, and spirit. Walking through the temple is the living scripture itself, enfolding the meanings of solar light, heat, air, and wind as shadows tell stories to the ones with eyes to see it. Pause for a moment and ponder how challenging a task it is to build a LIVING temple (temp = time, el = message); one that both holds and disseminates knowledge to the ones with ears to hear. Being with and in the rooms of this temple is the initiatory process itself and if you are attuned to nature, you'll get the correct answers which lead you to the correct questions, spiraling into the depths of true intention. This is the power of number when understood and used creatively.

The point here is, though the Viracochas are not Egyptian, Viracochas? I asked myself. I will figure this out and in so doing, discover that the transformation of one mask of deity into another appears in pattern in many different cultures, and more important that their obvious link is their oneness. They may be the same principle consciousness in multiple times and forms. I began to see this oneness as the way of the higher consciousness to generate or regenerate ever newness or growth. This is the mode of transformation of consciousness itself and why each moment is always new.

The infinite consciousness (the Nagual) in terms of numbers is oneness as being irreducible, it has no split or division, it's non-dual. And in the creation by it, man is born and he is still encoded oneness but is split or dual. He is dual because by design he is created as the density of matter (or mortal body) and the levity of spirit (or immortal aspect). Man is both but by his divine design encodes oneness, so he is the reducible one (as long as he has a physical body). Being reducible gives rise to the number 2, and duality is manifested. Now the manifestation of geometry can build into dimensions and this is why geometry is at the very least 3 dimensional and now we have the number 3. The trinity giving rise to form as we sense it by our bodies. The body of man will eventually be dissolved into earth, this is the reducible part of his oneness. Whereas God or infinite consciousness has no body and cannot be reduced, it is all that is. Seeing this is cosmo memetic; meaning we become a reflection of the universal consciousness itself. We understand finally we are directly in contact with reality itself.

"What is God? God is length, width, volume and death" -Saint Bernard

In order for me to understand who the Viracochas are, I see I must become whole because they are a myriad of differentiated cosmic principles that are all linked to the whole of human potential consciousness. If you see one of them alone, you see a fragment or hologram and understanding holograms you see each fragment holds or encodes all of its whole. A drop of dew reflects the entire universe within it, if you just look deeply into it, and human DNA encodes all the numbers and geometry of infinite consciousness, if you just have the vantage to see it. For those that intellectually or rationally deny this, think, and embody that if we did not encode this universality the words on this page would not exist and Schwaller de Lubicz would not have the aptitude to even present the idea. The existence of this concept gives rise to its potential reality. The word IDEA refers to co-creation itself. Idea =I dios, meaning the god within.

If you view the broken shards of a mirror from a fragmented approach, you will never see deeply enough to put them all back together as the whole. You must feel in order to see wholeness, the fire within the heart is the fuel for this. The fire keepers of sacred ground, ritual, and ceremony are those who still see the unity in consciousness. The Viracochas are teachers of this keeping of the fire within. If your culture is fragmented, you will know them by their lack of ability to feel, and they will be opposed to feeling themselves. They are afraid to feel. They must see that the only way to be a whole person is go into our dark emotions without judging, we must go into our shadow side in order to truly feel. You cannot feel by being in fear and in fear, you cannot or will not look into your shadow. The Viracochas teach how to see our dark emotions for what they really are. They teach us to burn the fire within and carry into the dark corners of our mind, the light we hold. It's a harmony we attune to. Just as the light of the sun reveals, it also conceals that which is behind it. The light can also blind. You cannot deny the beauty of the night and act as if you live in perpetual daylight.

The Viracochas or golden teachers have many names in transformed themselves to their spirit form or astral body while here on earth. They have learned to transcend mind or idea. Functioning from their center they still use mind and idea but are not driven or make decisions by it. I've been told that they, in this state, are sustained in their mortal body by immortal light consciousness. And in so, they teach that in this state of grace, it's the heart which has deep knowing and truth, not the mind. And that the mind is not a creator, it is a processor and organizer, the heart alone embodies the live current suitable for creating.

The heart, organized as 7 muscle types in key vibration is always more reliable than the mind. It is a deeper more ancient and intuitive knowing while the mind is a process of learning or learning how to know. The heart generates an Elysian field which is man's luminous cocoon, some say it is his being. The field, or luminous cocoon, functions just as the cosmos does so it has magnetic polarity as well as the law of correspondence as well as the law of as above so below. So in this way the heart is intimately linked with the entire universe or cosmos and brings into the body of man the celestial bodies and primarily our solar system at the time of birth and throughout man's life. In this solar system, all of its movements and energies are constantly falling, arcing, or gravitating as celestial dew toward a center focal point.

In our small solar system we are reliant on and powered by our sun for life and consciousness here on earth. The human body is comprised the same way, there is a focal point where all of these energies, electric and magnetic, converge this focal point in the seat of man's highest self-awareness. It is the golden bodies of the Bodhisattva for the Buddha. When man truly harmonizes his being with this cosmic order his physical body glows and radiates with light as it is now harmonized with this golden body his highest self. The golden light occurs because in order to harmonize man's body with these orders, he has to learn to center himself within the vibration of heart because the cosmos itself and creation itself is created to a purpose of progress, growth, and love. For creation...It should be known, that theses Viracochas and the highest of the ancient wisdom keepers, are the brilliant Ascended Masters who have harmonized into their golden luminous bodies, through the heart. But it should be known that they have transcended mind which means they no longer rest in ideas but are so attuned to the current moment that their apprehension of reality is what is powering their being.

There are many who will intellectualize, criticize, and argue that the universe is not created by benevolence or love. But when speaking with the golden ones and the beings that have transcended mind and sustain their bodies by light alone, they will tell you that this is in fact the case. Love ultimately is the first and sustaining impetus of creation because love does not demand. Love always bestows and is benevolent for the greater good. Basically the universe or creation is sustaining itself in constant energetic growth and flux for its own greatest good. If this were not true, we would not have a moment of self-awareness. The universe is constantly going through creation and destruction but we have an awareness of a life span that is all about growth, growth in the mind, body, psyche, and soul. This is our awareness of the greater good moving to and through benevolence in love in creation. We are divine beings.

We see this through certain emotions dying in man as his consciousness ascends. Certain emotions always accompany this process of growth. Namely the benevolent emotions are always present when you are around a holy person for someone who is ascending or has ascended and is sustaining their golden body of light. For example, these beings always have the emotion of compassion, benevolence, charity, understanding, and the most appreciation for his or her relationship to existence. Think about this, these are the marks of the highest forms that man can ascend to. This is why we follow enlightened beings, this is why we follow angelic beings, the light itself is encoded and designed for this process of growth and awareness

As selfishness cannot grow, unselfishness absolutely can. And power in general is the built-in force that accompanies man, and actually guides him in this self-awareness growth maneuver. As power accompanies him, he grows but understands that all these patterns of growth cannot be found in the mind they are patterns of the heart.

As for the ancient thread of connection of these beings to a higher archetypal source, it is hard to pin down the thread. Here we can research into some wise men, sages, and rishis and peek into this mystery. Though there are subtle differences in each pining point of this thread, the ancients are in agreement that the thread exists and its purpose is the incarnation of higher consciousness into the earth for the ascension of humans. For example, it is said that the Norse God Wotan or Woden or Odin is the same being who inhabited the body known as the Buddha. Also, some say they are all Hearne, Hermes Trismegistus, and Thoth. Even the Buddha himself is rumored to acknowledge this archetypal light with him. Christ is of this lineage however, there is a difference in him, although it seems to lie only in the western sages, so I am uncertain of its testimonial. I will highlight it, but reader be of open mind and esoteric thought so as to fully grasp the meaning and significance in this mystery. It is not to be taken lightly or judged hastily. Suggestion says, sit with it and meditate upon it before making up your mind.

It is as follows: First understand the occult teachings to the Atlantean, Egyptian, and Druidic initiates. The cosmic principles of subtle light bodies, before man was developed into the hardened physical bodies he is today, were personified as Osiris, Horus, and Isis. Osiris was not a physical body as we think today, he was a combination of astral, ethereal, and physical. All manifested by vibrations of light densities. He was a physical body but not so dense to have bones and heavy organs. Many angelic beings are still this way today. He was intimately attached to the light of sun reflected by the moon, so he is ruled by the moon. As the sun and moon moved further away from each other he was opposed by his unruly brother Set and was killed by him and cut into 14 pieces. But his sister and wife (Isis) secretly retrieved these pieces and put them back together. This is why the moon's phases wax and wane in segments of 14, they are the aspects of Osiris still regulating human rhythms on earth today.

The point here is really that man, today has been the culmination of solar and celestial forces of light evolution. Understand that man's original body was not physically dense, but physical light, much like a cloud of gas in a star nursery. Gradually by movements on the systems through the galaxy his consciousness has evolved to what we perceive today. This is why the sun and moon have always been worshiped as gods or beings. They still power our subtle bodies, and affect our consciousness. The human body is so physically dense today that we often lose awareness of our soul and subtle bodies. The ego came into us as we became physical as well, and gave us our independent nature of individuality. This is a necessary step in the equilibrium of being; the balance of being in a dense body that will die and a soul eternal. The divine ego is an equalizer of this paradox.

So on to the Christ event. The christus consciousness may be in the line of incarnated Viracochas as I have learned it so. This consciousness choosing to enfold itself in a dense body on the material earth, came here to shift reality for all the earth. Its difference from the other Viracochas is said to be that when it entered into the body of Jesus of Nazareth (of the branch) a change of density occurred. The bones (being the densest organs of the body) dissolved or shifted into a subtle light. The body evolved and quickened. As evolutions of bodies have developed certain organs over eons, the functions and being have evolved too, creating a symbiotic bio feedback loop within the being itself. The development of man's bony structures dovetails with his deeper independence. The harder his body became, the greater the power of death influences his consciousness. The harder he becomes, the less he remembers his immortal soul. The conscious Christ being extended and penetrated into the bones of the body, chemically changing them and the entire body.

Deeply understand the significance of this event, for it established on Earth a supremacy over death, in a human body. See, through aeons of development, man's bodies have been evolving and when the bones appeared from gelatinous cartilage, into incredible hardness, death outshined his consciousness of his immortal soul. Much like a baby in the womb, as he has a watery supple body he has no individuality or knowledge of death. Upon birth, he slowly becomes a harder body, as he ages his bones become more dense thus resulting in individual ego consciousness and predominance of his inevitable death. For most of us, it is the death event or disintegration of the physical body that awakens us once again to our union with the eternal immortal.

The Christ event marks the supremacy over death here on Earth, here in the material body. At the least, it marks a permanent shift in the psyche and hopefully the souls of all humans to realize we are spiritual beings, even if we are in a physical world. This does not mean that all people need to call themselves Christians, as all the Viracochas are incarnations of the crystal consciousness. They incarnate here curtailed in each being, at the appropriate time, in the way for the greatest potential spiritual evolution. It is important to see that man's needs, impetuous, impulses, are all unique to the current reality, situation, and time. This is the event of deepest spiritual evolution.

Deeper we go into the Christ mystery. As the being of Christ took the body and fused it with the supremacy over death we see cosmic forces again. The osiris, Isis, myth gives birth to their son Horus, who is the SUN. The Christ being is also bound in the sun, as the son. Earth, and moon are all interdependent. The light of the being we call the sun (Christ) is the power and sustainer of the earth itself and life upon it. So, the solar light, which regulates life, incarnated into the man known as Jesus (iosus). The solar being now directly influencing the earth from its surface, the being walks among the earth's fields, making immortal consciousness known. The blood of people is also affected, as we know the sun regulates not only the chemistry of the foods that man ingests but also the chemical wedding of man himself. Without the sun, man's sight, sleep, dream, metabolism, and consciousness disappears. In this event, in this way, the new blood is born in man, on earth. The ramifications are a plethora. Just think, as man's consciousness evolves into higher states of benevolence, thus so his actions and stewardship of the earth, his home. As man awakens, ascends, the planet heals and holds him sweeter, for she is conscious as well. She is bound in energy and rhythm to the sun since her creation. So this Christ event strengthens the bond of sun, moon, and earth

As man becomes aware of his immortal spirit, his life, time, and culture change. He slowly becomes aware of his spirit bodies in sleep and can work on himself as he leaves his body when he sleeps at night. He can attune himself so much as to work on himself upon his death. His immortal nature does not have to be unconscious when he leaves his body at death. Just as in sleep he can be lucid and conscious. This is why the ancient Egyptians developed mummification of their sacred bodies. They knew the body is the temple of God, and thus housing the immortal. They preserved their body in time, so the soul with its consciousness in death would have the opportunity to recognize the body and the sacred knowledge learned while in it. The Egyptians, and the rishis of India, were practicing christ consciousness long before the Nazarene put his feet upon the sea. Man has always had physical, astral, and ethereal bodies but did not develop them enough to be conscious until descent into bone-dense physicality. And this ego works on the evolution of spirit just as the higher physical, astral and ethereal bodies work on his spirit. It is sort of a ping-pong up and down the light waves of consciousness, for the purpose of evolution. These are designed for the highest potential and greatest benefit. A body's, organs, and structure are as they are because of this evolution and refinement.

So we see that the mysterious line of Viracochas, and some not mentioned here are the divine beings incarnate here for the betterment of all mankind. They have not hidden this from us. We were to unconscious to see them or remember our own divinity reflected by them. Many modern people will call this fantasy, just as they do of myth. But look deeper and see the long lasting myths have more to tell us than a short story. If you only grasp the story, you have not grasped anything at all, except a few names. But what is in a name? Like symbols, they encode, and enfold light, light full of layers of meaning originally told to speak to the souls of men, to the ears of men. As with us beautiful creatures, us humans, there is much more than meets the eye. There is the, I am. There is the sun in our hearts, our solar plexus, and the moon in our heads. There is Isis, Osiris, and Horus still beaming light down into us.

Mistakes in thinking or mistakes in the mind can be corrected and the course redirected towards growth but understand that the heart has a deeper knowing and the ultimate connection to man's golden, luminous body of light. The connection to light itself must not be destroyed. He must understand that to pervert the heart is his greatest self-destruction. This is defaming of the temple of God, which is his physical body. If he twists and corrupts the heart badly enough, the temple or body will die, just as if he harmonizes with the cosmic order, the grand architect of love, he may organize his own luminous body to ride the waves of the immortal spirit in eternity.

And onward, looking deep into the mystery teachings of the line of Viracochas, I speak of the druidic initiations in ancient Hibernia. Here they taught to the initiate of the trinitized, balance between dualities. These masters spoke of male energies being akin to that we call science, which lacks being. And the female energies being akin to art and fantasy, which lacks truth. The lack in both can only be united in the WORD, as in the beginning of all creation was the word. The sovereign word of your soul is what transcends them both, creating something always new, called unity. As bodies and forms are constantly being disintegrated and annihilated, so is unity constantly being integrated and created. Identity with annihilation is surrender to the current moment as identity with creation is harmony in perpetual growth. The

WORD here is the cosmic Christ principle and it is man's duty to find meaning in the knowledge he has gathered. If he fails at this duty he has gathered no knowledge at all, he has only acquired, images and pictures lacking in truth and being.

6

Emotion: Energy in Motion

've struggled with my body for as long as I can recall. In very early childhood I fought for my right at the table (so to speak). What I mean is, violence as a way to solve problems was handed down and taught to me from my environment and some of those around me. As I became an adult I gradually became aware of this. My body literally told me. As a boy the culture of the southern American is coined as a culture of honor and it is. Southerners value honor, fortitude, and independence, especially in a male. This indeed is a beautiful sentiment when in the correct context but it also has a yang side, it also has some consequences. Namely, one has to either be tough or make people believe they are tough; otherwise you will be stricken down by verbal, physical, or emotional abuse. As a child I learned quickly how to talk, fight, and defend what I wanted and this is what I thought was normal and good.

When, in other cultures, as I have seen in many other countries, they value other things. Slowly I began to see the faults in my psychology. I had stored programs in my deep subconscious mind that constantly fed my conscious mind and then of course projected my view of reality. These programs act as mind states, value bases, claimed knowledge. For me, it was like looking through rose colored glasses only mine were more dimly brown. I was an accomplished athlete as a boy, it was liberating and fun. Also it served as a means to express my fortitude in my culture and claim my honor, but it only served my soul up to a certain point. It fell short when my programs and perceptions of reality started to crack and fall apart. This is a life crisis, and most people go through it at some stage, for me it was at age nineteen. My identity began to molt. A very powerful and unique sage channeled the spiritual light of the god force and I saw for the first time, a reality that shattered my perceptions and my identification with them. Luminous beings full and emanating bright light appeared in front me. Clearly they were not she, the channel. Light features slowly pulse and emanate from within her, it appears that she disappears and they appear. The emanations are to me a realm that is unfiltered by my previous limited perception. The light bodies of the spirit world are seeing me and connecting in some language without words. Some were male with beards, and one was female. My life and soul has been changed from that moment on. It is not something one can dismiss or forget.

My body has been in pain, imbalance, and sometimes dreadful agony for most of my days. I've been keenly aware it. When I was five and six years old my soccer coach would constantly teach me to use my left foot on the ball but I never would. It was frustrating for him, he must have thought I was a stubborn little tyrant. But this went on for the rest of my athletic life. It wasn't that I didn't want to use the left foot, the problem was I really couldn't. I tried and remember my body just not doing what I asked, I had a disconnection and couldn't command it to perform. So I became very good with the right side of my body, in all endeavors.

Over time, I became severely imbalanced and have spent over twenty years correcting the issue. As before, my body has been speaking to me all along, only I was too steeped in arrogance and honor to listen. The body is truly the temple, the temple of God. Not a temple, THE temple. The body is the only thing in life that humans ever really possess or own. It is uniquely stamped with your one of a kind signature. When we die, we relinquish it to the ground, the grandmother spirit. Nothing we buy or purchase will we ever own or take with us upon death, and so its value is completely transitory and material. The body is a vibratory manifestation directed by the subconscious mind, it is our subconscious mind in physical expression, and it's talking to us all the time. It will reflect your state of health, energy, and awareness. It took me years of intellectual thinking about my painful and chronic condition before I understood that my emotional state was expressing itself in the physical body. I had no idea that my emotions could enliven or debilitate health in the body. Why didn't I know this? It's not because I was stupid, it's because in my culture, no ever told me. No one knew or valued this perspective, they had too much pride. This only became apparent for me as I came to know a beautiful and caring woman, named Carly. She had been through her own battles with the body and learned how emotions affect the system. Over time she taught me to see this grand insight through her feminine beauty and mind.

And now I see why I have so many female teachers in my life. I've been unable to use my left side correctly due to a spiritual, emotional, and energetic imbalance. Low and behold as a holistic approach to manhood, I absolutely require a good and balanced woman.

Carly also introduced me to another wonderful woman, her name is Shelly. I became open to trying a healing session of craniosacral therapy with her based on Carly's referral. I also knew this type of work was potentially profound based on my time and experience with horses. I was in doubt about the modality of healing until I saw it performs on the sacred equine. They don't lie like people do. Horses are authentic reflectors of their emotional states. Upon witnessing a horse during a craniosacral session I knew something profound was at work. I decided to commit to this and go see Shelly. I recorded my sessions with Shelly.

Craniosacral Therapy: Documenting emotional body release 12/20/13-

As I lay there on the table she holds my head and face or puts her hands on my chest. I feel extreme tension within my body in familiar places. My neck, sacrum, groin, pelvis and hamstring are like knotted twine. I feel it move, get stronger and weaker, like the tides flowing in and out. As I focus on breathing into these points of pain, a flood of images rushes to the forefront of my mind. They appear like leaves falling from autumn trees. She can't see what I am seeing but she somehow knows there is a point of reference, something is happening. She instructs me to focus my attention on what I see and breathe into it for clarity. I do.

These are some of the clear emotional states and images that bubbled to the surface during my experience: My body as a baby and possibly in utero is feeling violence. The violence causes discomfort and confusion. It causes me to contract deep in my core in a survival response. I am aware of my core, the spaces around my spine, from genitals to neck to chest and armpits in severe contraction. I am so small, I am helpless. The emotional contraction moves my physical body within the soft tissue structures that hold my muscular/skeletal integrity; the fascia. The fascia responds to the fear state, the fight or flight state that I am in. My core is in a holding pattern of pain and survival. I need unwinding! I need expansion, I need release. I don't learn this until many years later. My body holds this pattern throughout my life. It remembers violence, then helplessness, then supreme confusion, then anger, then pain. I carry these with me into my developing young identity.

My baby body's natural state is not this; it is resting, peaceful, safe, and warm. Back on the table with her it becomes clear to me that my baby body is just that. I sort of went back to my baby state with my emotions. Not long after I was born the violence began, which clouded the open and natural state. I realize now the dreams of the dying baby girls are an aspect of myself; it's my feminine side. My female-intuitive energy was dying and I carried it across that canal to feel its pain, save it, and love it. It's my little self. We all are a delicate balance of both feminine (magnetic) and masculine (electric) energies. The more out of balance they are the more we suffer. I feel a very strong sense of needing help. I cry…help, help. I am so small. In the arms of a mother I am fine, I am safe. However, this I believe only made the violence worse because when I am not in the protecting arms of mom, I am alone.

The power of threat. The threat of violence. As an adult I see this causes more confusion and teaches me violence. As now I know I carry violence with me. My culture and environment were also teaching me violence as a young boy. School was rough and competitive. Anger became my form of protection. I used this violence in sports it made me aggressive and also egocentric. I lost my healthy body to injury and pain at age 19 and I believe I lost it for the purpose of spiritual growth. The violence paradigm began to serve me less and less. Still, now at age 37, I struggle with letting go of it, just how to do it. How will I protect myself if I am attacked? Will I resort back to fight or flight mode. I believe I will if I am cornered.

This is truly what came bubbling up from within me during this therapy. I realize that tiptoeing around this conversation with myself will not suffice. If I ignore this event it will only hinder me further in my growth and healing. I understand. My baby body had no way of understanding, it only absorbed. My adult body understands. I am not blaming, I am going through to heal, to heal deep within. The violence came up again from before I was born. It came to me as a shortcoming from the times of my ancestors' frustration with their lives. An ancestral vision like memory appeared in pictures. I believe our grandfathers' grandfathers coped with many things by using taught violence. The struggles of their lives to survive in their times were not easy for them. They pushed their way through things, and when times got rough I think they got angry. I see grimace and tight-jaw teeth grinding their souls away while holding arthritic fists filled with loss and lies. Our father has felt this in his childhood as well, however he chose a different form of communication with it. He genuinely chose to make it better, despite what was dealt to him as a little one. It is all here, now, reflecting in us, crystallizing and annihilating us. We will do even better. Our ancestors were taught anger and violence, they had to grin and bear it. My baby body, my temple will consciously evolve. I will do even better.

I also saw you and I in another time and place. I am speaking of my older brother Ian. More images visit me. Our soul connection may be older than we know. I witness us in fierce competition in another life. Or what I think is another life. We were yelling and screaming at each other in front of others in a green and dark room. Frothing and pointing fingers at the beginnings of rage. I guess you asked me to show up here, this time around for some deeper reason. It may be to resolve our competitions and violence and put them to rest once and for all. I don't know what to make of all this...It was once covered but now coming to the surface.

There's more. I have a need to tell. I've been aware of this for a while within my internal dialogue and still don't really understand it, this is my attempt. I often tell myself of how I am going to tell my story. It's like I am watching myself interview myself to an accepting audience. The audience is me (loving and accepting myself). I talk to myself in this way and think it's strange, but I find myself doing it. I think it's really my emotional body healing itself. In some ways (not all), My creative expression (art, drawing, painting, writing, music) is my emotional body needing to tell someone about my pain. Me holding pain. It is the need to be whole, it's therapeutic.

My baby body, my little open soul dipped in violence, cracked a bit and this reflected in the body. This left my soul energy partly fragmented. There was a day when I felt I could have left this body behind and move back to spirit. I was dry and withering from within, like a plant with no water. I had a choice, I chose to stay here in this body and rebuild. I am rebuilding. The fragmented soul energy began its re-entry into the body that day. I have been reintegrating ever since. I am learning to heal, to unwind and expand out of a long contraction. My baby body needs safety, love, and to hold peace. I am exhausted.

Session 2 with Shelly Rike :

More and more violence came through as one of the primary blockers of my success with the healing of my body. My adult body has been riddled with myalgia/neuralgia of some sort for at least twenty years. As I dig deeper into pain in the body I realize that from an early age I have felt symptoms of it. I remember athletics at age eleven or so and having soft tissue pain in the upper thighs when I ran. This happened suddenly one day during a game. The coach and my mother thought I was acting or faking it to avoid playing a certain position on the field, but I wasn't. I was shocked and confused as to the sudden new feeling in my legs. It gradually went away but not completely. I've lived with it, and assumed it was just due to puberty or changes in my chemistry.

When I was around age five or six, I was pressured into going up to a little boy named Tee and starting a fight with him. I didn't want to hurt him or anyone else but it was something I did because I was pushed into it by my peer. I didn't want to let him down and I didn't want to seem weak, so with him backing me up, I went to fight this boy. I basically antagonized him with name calling and such and at some point kicked him a few times with my tiny cowboy boots. He submitted and we left prideful and victorious. All little kids do these things and it doesn't seem like much. However as I grow, I realized I have a pattern of violence in in my life. My brother and I have had anger programed into us since we were small and it's a program that elicits a nervous system response of fight or flight. As with little Tee, I knew I didn't want to hurt him, I didn't want to lose him as a friend or potential friend. There was a part of me that shifted when I gave in to being violent for the sake of boasting or acting tough. Tee may have been a brat, I don't really know, but he was a person that I hurt. I opened myself to being mean and when I did, there was a part of me that knew it was against my true core nature. I realize now that I let myself down by fragmenting my core nature of childhood joy, by not saying no to that battle.

These craniosacral sessions are uncovering why I have had so much pain in my body for so long. I have been stuck in a fight or flight response (emotionally) since my childhood. It even affected my ideas about raising a family of my own. I am just not ready to raise a child and I know it's because of multiple factors. One of those factors is that I don't want to pass on this pattern to my own child, so I am healing myself first. I am breaking the pattern and reprograming to something that better serves me! I have so many personal conflicts in my life, I can't even remember them all. I kicked a kid in the throat one day on a trampoline. I fought a friend in front of the entire neighborhood once. That was some serious pressure. I was rough in every sport I played. I was kicked in the ribs while fighting a stranger. He attacked me for no reason whatsoever and I had no choice but to fight as he was on top of me before I knew it. I had no chance of flight (to run), I absolutely had to protect and defend myself. My ribs have never been the same. In later years, I fought in a bar with a boxing ring for the potential to win a prize. I even have dreams of fighting people, struggling to punish them. The point is, my autonomic nervous system has been in a heightened protection/survival mode for most of my life. I am now learning how unhealthy this is for me. During the session, Shelly was working on my ribs (she knew something was wrong there, without me telling her). My emotional state went back to that moment of being attacked by a complete stranger. She and I could feel my inner organs shaking/trembling just from remembering the event. It was uncontrollable. The body remembers and stores these emotional events in the soft tissue and working through them is what I have to do to heal.

Moving on...More comes up. I had a feeling of uneasiness when my father came into my thoughts. I realize he may have been given the same violent and selfish program when he was a child. He may have been given even more harmful ones too. I know he left home at a young age and didn't have the desire to return. Stories tell me this is due to the way his father treated him. These types of patterns in my family are ancestral in my belief. I think times for the poor starving Irish were hard indeed, and this is a part of my family heritage. We are survivors for certain but when times get better we need to get better ourselves. We ought to devote our will and spirit not to conquer and conflict but to peace and healing. I cast no blame to anyone as I am here/now and blessed to be responsible for my own soul and its enlightenment.

Since my father was a victim of verbal, emotional, and even physical abuse at times in his childhood, this is probably why he doesn't really speak to his father and has a very minimal relationship with him. We all have our own path to healing, and what may be most important in this process may be just showing up to engage and do the work. A child shunned, dominated, pointed at in blame, does not forget! We remember so well that we carry the emotionality with us day in and day out. We often don't even know that we know these things but are designed to use them as a staircase to true health. I will not carry a program of victimhood simply because it serves no greater good. It only holds us back and slows growth to the true nature of us; we are something good and beautiful. I will not give that pattern to another because it only harms myself.

Deep in thought one day, somewhat like a vivid daydream. It was a day between the craniosacral sessions. Often remnants of insight from them would come to me. My hand propping up my head, window blinds letting in just the right amount of sunshine in the wind. I had been pondering the body and the temple. My awareness is shifting daily, synchronistically. I found in many ancient cultures the reverence for the glands and the endocrine system within the body. In Egypt the major temples along the river Nile were built in correspondence with the glands of the human body; a map on earth as a reflection of the cosmic order of the heavens. The Egyptians, they knew something important, so important they spent thousands of years creatively encoding it into the people, culture, and architecture.

They called the fluid or oil that is produced in the

higher glands of the brain, (namely the cerebrum) krast. The oil, thousands of years later in Greece is called christus, or oil. This oil is produced in part by the pituitary gland and partly by the pineal gland. One feminine, the other masculine. This physical physiology is profound and far reaching in the mind, being, and consciousness of man. The pituitary is a primary regulator of the overall health of the body. Its chemical secretions combined with others can produce tremendous physical growth and aging of the body. It's also linked to smell. The pineal regulates the growth of awareness or consciousness in the being within the body. As a child's consciousness and cognition differ from that of an adult and that of the aged, the pineal controls the waves of ascent and descent in the body.

These are the master glands of the body where in consciousness and body are in equilibrium. Both consciousness and psychic energy are distributed throughout the body. So in the pineal, consciousness and body merge and in pituitary, psychic and body merge. Furthermore, psychic and psychological aberrations can be traced to the feminine pituitary body while awareness can be traced to the masculine pineal. Clarity of psychosis is the process between the two oils. Their energies as they generate a mixture that runs the length of the spine and entire system, urges them back to the cerebrum in a new formulation; the genesis of balance between the masculine and the feminine in the holy temple, the body and its chakras.

The pituitary responds primarily and primordially to order, and smells are created by subtle vibration. The burning of incenses for example is a vibratory event. As the gland responds to odor, it has a tremendous effect on the body, when obtuse it can cause the body to become extremely fat or very thin. Also, when the event is acute it seems to heighten the body's psychic ability. As I became more acquainted with the body and its sacred oils, my awareness shifted. I became more sensitive to my emotional body and working with it. I went back to Shelly for another session. This one brought up feelings of my mother.

After the session I spoke with my mother and shared with her this. Something deep and informative came up for me today in my 4th cranio sacral session. As I unwind my energy/emotional body I am led to hold a spot of tension and breathe through it. My neck tight and slowly softening, a spot of pain I've been holding on to for many years. It brings me back to when I was around four years old. I was so sad...

Only thing is I had no way to know why I was sad. My little boy brain was still in a theta (brainwave state). This means I only sponged or took in stimulus, felling, and knowledge; I did process it. Our emotional state as children seems to be something we spend our entire adult life processing, and that's what I am doing now. My sadness comes from you and dad splitting, it's the loss of balance in my feminine and masculine sides of my energy/emotional body (the part of me that is empathic/feels). This imbalance has led me through many life changes that I believe manifested in my bodily pain and injuries I've been carrying all these years. There is no blame in this letter, only acknowledgment and heart love.

See, all these years I thought your divorce didn't really affect me, I figured I was too young to really remember. Turns out, I was wrong. My energetic sensitivity was functioning even at age two or three. My memory goes back to a photo of Ian and I, one I truly like and is a great photo. We are together as brothers and bonded even then for life. The picture turned out good but the moment it was taken was rough for me. Ian and I were out in the backyard waiting for the photo to be taken so of course we were playing. But we were alone and really fighting. The actual fight I don't remember, but the feeling I had in the photo, I do. Ian had just pushed me around and I felt his aggression and frustration shoved my way. He was only trying to process the loss of his father and mother himself.

I was crying when you came out to take the picture and didn't know what had transpired but wanted to take the picture. I was told to quit crying and dry my eyes and get ready for the picture. And, then I did. The photo is a good one and captures brothers bonded, but also captures my sadness. When I see that photo and some others too, I see the water still welled up in my little eyes. It's like at the moment the picture was finished I flooded my cheeks again. I feel the pit in my throat of holding back tears still to this day. Only now my adult mind processes these tears as tears of love, for you.

The day dad left I could feel his sadness, he was truly hurt. I remember that day and watching him drive away. No processing yet, only feeling; feeling of hurt and sadness. Over the years I had your story and his and this is not about who said what. It's about the imbalance of female/male emotionality. From age three I've been imbalanced. All my injuries have been from head to toe on my left side, which is the feminine side. I wondered about that for years. As an athlete, even a very young one, my coaches always told me to use my left foot in soccer. I never did. Reason being, I couldn't. I really had very little coordination with it or control over it. However my right side was very good, very agile, and very strong. I managed to become a good athlete at most sports primarily with my right side. I knew this throughout my soccer career but didn't develop my left side despite what my coaches and training asked of me.

Because I was a boy and felt my father's hurt, I sided with him. I basically believed his story. All the details don't really matter, what matters is I wanted to be tough because I was a boy. I wanted to be a man because I had a big brother like Ian. I wanted to be able to fight because of the abusive environments that were around me. I wanted to be a strong man, even when I was a little boy, a little sensitive energetic being. It's not that I didn't believe your story too, it's that I felt dad's pain and wanted be a man so I followed his and Ian's lead on how to do that.

You have told me I've been very independent from early on, that this was my stoic disposition. I have also been told and feel that I often distanced myself from your affection. I remember the emotion of pulling away from you as a little boy. I don't know if you remember it this way. I was told that Ian always asked for your attention/affection and I mostly did not. I am sure I accepted when I needed it but often times I pushed away. The reason is because I grew up emotionally focused on my right side (the masculine side). I did this because my father was hurt and gone. I leaned more towards his story than yours. Now I don't. I understand your choices as a mother were nurturing and in the best interest of your children. You were looking out for us all the time.

I feel that the destructive nature of your divorce also put you and dad in a survival state emotionally. You both had pain and high stress. If you were in a high stress state I think Ian and I sponged it and learned it too. My tears of love I am feeling in this moment are for you. I've realized I've held you at some kind of safe distance for most of my life. I have not opened and loved you to a full capacity. I am learning! I am so sorry I've withheld love from you. I am returning all that to you now. I love you! I am happy now as a MAN to understand that I continually need your love and support. I am learning to receive it.

Why this is hard for me to express I chalk up to my male/female energetic imbalance. I imagine you a little girl getting balanced love as you needed it, you only know for sure. My unwinding in the body has a process of emotion. For years I never even considered the idea that my 20 year left side struggle could have anything to do with emotion. There is healing within us and I am tapping into mine, and it's' going to be my story it tells. It's not your story or dad's story that I require any more, (what made me pick sides). This is the bigger story, one of how we heal. The pulling away I have within me is because of hurt, abuse, and sadness. I am loving you now in a greater capacity which brings me more to balance.

Your son-

As time traverses my mind and heart, each day after these experiences I become more aware of my emotional state, I have small memories come up to teach me something about myself, my family, my upbringing. I feel my body shift here and there in the right way, I know I am releasing and in a process of letting go. I also am so knowing of how powerful our mind and emotions can be. These memories that percolate are coming from my subconscious mind and being handed to my conscious mind because I must be ready to deal with them. Each day I progress.

One night after a very long day of study, horsemanship, and work, I found myself instantly asleep, as soon as my pillow allowed my head to fall upon it. I dreamt. I was lucid as I know who I am and what I am doing in the dream. I am in the backseat of a car, it's dark and dim. There are two others there and my mother is in front, driving. She is sobbing and expressing a heavy burden of guilt for something deep inside her. Something she has been hiding for a long time. She is so heavy with emotional pain she pulls out a small pistol and begins to place it under her chin, points it as if she may take her own life. The air in my lungs and in the car is thick and fearful. We all have a reaction of gentle yet high alertness. I speak something of compassion, although I can't recall the words. They were more like feeling I was caressing her ears with. As I spoke I slowly wrapped my fingers around the gun and gently opened her hand to let it go. She did and I moved the gun away and back toward my window in the back. I rolled it down and pointed it out the window, knowing I was doing a great thing. The next thing I know I am in a house with two other people, they are familiar but I don't know them. My dream construction didn't need the details of their identity to be relevant. I ask about a forbidden room within the house. He replies "do you want to go to see it? It's a mysterious darkness?" I am lead to the hidden door. It seems like junky timbers of wood about half the size in length of a normal door opening. It's got other pieces of wood just a few inches inside and then a few more, like ribs or layers to enter. They block a view in, if there was a vantage point to see inside, it's absurd by theses timbers of wood. As I fearfully look at the opening, my anxiety rises fast. I look at the person who led me there, and he is turning the corner to leave the room we are in. I hurry towards his shadow beyond the corner but he is gone. He left as if he wanted nothing to do with the situation. I wanted to follow him towards a feeling of safety but then the hair on my chest stood up and I realize I am alone and the opening to the dark door knows I am there. It was as if the door was already open and I had to face its consequences.

Now I am seriously frightened and then remember this feeling of intense worry and fear from another dream in which I was in a secret room within another house. This other house was much bigger and no one who lived there would ever go into the room. The room was very large and had twists and turns and levels within it there were unseen until you found them. It's a strange setting of things or spaces of things lost and very heavy when found. It's an emotion that I don't know how to describe, it's scary but still. It's pervasive and taps into anyone who is within the space of the room. Also it seems as if when in there, you have a feeling of being lost, very lost, like you don't know where you are or where you're going. Even so, it's like the room transports you to places outside; the wilderness or a backyard somewhere but you're still inside the house in the labyrinth of the hidden room.

I have these squealing feelings of anxiety as I look at the door, it's got no handle, it's just a dark, narrow, hole in the wall. I pause and lean downward to look inside the door and its just darkness, I cannot see inside. Since I am in a dream, instead of squinting to procure my view, I pull out a light. I pulled out a round light like a flare, like one you would use when out at sea at night. The light is bright in my hand and like a small torch sun, it's maneuverable and wielding. I lean it in, and it pulses its luminosity and I see the beam shine in and cannot make out any features but see the beam travel far inside. I know the door opens to a large room. I am still terrified and decide I don't want to go inside. It's just an emotion of the anticipation of a dark feeling in there that I am not ready to have laid upon me. I immediately realize the power of my beheld light, I can see in the room I am in and now; at least see the dark door light up. I am electrified with this insight. I now hold a light and I didn't bring it in the dream with me, I simply created it. I bestowed it upon myself and its presence is hugely significant. I now have and hold my own shining light. I feel the power to see that which is around me, the power to direct it on things I want and look at with clarity. It's like having clarity at your fingertips.

Still feeling the anxiety of the room, I elect not to venture in. But I have the keen insight of the nature of the dream world. I magically created my light from within, I gave it to myself from the imagination. I know now that the dream world has natural laws that are of different physics than the waking world. I have a sense of creative power and knowledge in the dream world. It's from within ourselves that the world's reality reveals itself. I see myself and my roles in life differently now. I begin to feel the stirrings of the waking world. I feel my bed and body lying there. I am aware of both realms now simultaneously, the dream and waking state, the tonal and the nagual, the temporary body and the infinite self. I begin to pray. I pray to the great spiritual masters who have enlightened themselves and ascended beyond the flesh body and into the light body or beyond. I've seen these masters come through Antoinette, I know they are real and I know they look after my well-being. I pray to the christ within, the christ consciousness, the yogi's of bhagavan Krishna, mahavatar babaji, Yogananda, swami Sri Yukteswar, the great grandmother spirit, and tunkashila, and to the great masters of light.

I feel tension in my body shifting and moving and twitching as I lay there in my bed. I know this feeling; it's the same shifts that occur in craniosacral sessions when the subconscious mind is bubbling up to the conscious mind that which it's ready to assimilate. The emotions of healing are happening, even the dark and scary ones. I observed them and see how my body transforms. I have warmth melting away tension in my fascia, I have twitching in my mid back and sacral spine, and I feel a balancing unfolding. I see light in a new way, I see the sun and I know why it's the God of the earthly peoples, I know why the ancients were so wise and why the sun light bestows life.

Without the light, our being would be hindered. Every aspect of our physical body is affected by the sun. All senses. We see everything on this planet because the sun's light illuminates the objects and effects of this physical place. Imagine being in darkness, imagine having no sun. We would never see at all. We would freeze to death, never give birth, never regenerate, never feel warmth, never have food to eat or water to drink. As light shines upon darkness, darkness fades to reveal reality and its vibratory effects.

Our thoughts are also affected by sunlight. The more light we have in our world the more clarity we potentially see, the higher and more evolved thinking we do, the more we bathe in the truth of what is. The sun's physical, spiritual, and psychic energy powers us all. The light I gave myself in the dream now serves me in the non-sleeping world because I see the dark door with light cast upon it. I don't know what subconscious emotion lies within that room but when I find out, I will bring the courage of the creative lamp with me to see it in the light. My body shifts; my palette, my throat, my sinus, my sacrum, my neck, and stomach all shake involuntarily. I just observe as the vibration of emotional healing rumbles through me like a sine wave.

Lakota Winds--

Autumn, just after frank's passing

Tara,

I trust this letter finds you in good health, good heart, and in a loving place...

I went to a ceremony of healing yesterday; it is a Native American ceremony that I attend from time to time. It is called a sweat lodge and has been practiced as a way of purification for hundreds, if not thousands of years. They are very intense and force you into a meditative state, a place of prayer and centeredness. This one in particular was very powerful for me and I know it's because of the Lakota medicine man who leads the lodge. His name is Lee Plentywolf and I connected with him deeply. He is a strong and gentle soul with years of clarity and wisdom.

In there it is completely dark, very hot, and filled with drumming, chanting, and singing. As of the past few months my emotional state has been shaky and so I found myself crying to let some pain out. Pain I've gone through, and pain you've gone through, and pain my family has gone through. As I opened up, I felt immense gratitude for being a part of my family, I am truly blessed to be in this moment, in this family; we are good people.

An image of your father (Uncle Frank to me) came to me clearly and he was smiling or more like grinning. He scratched his beard and was chuckling, not laughing but chuckling, as if he knew something special and was at ease. It's very hard to describe this in words, but he has a way about him, a disposition of always being ready to laugh. So he was chucking and gave me a message. It was only few words but I want to share them with you and the family. He said "There is no reason to get yourself wound up, it's easy and natural...like when the wind blows". He repeated this over and over, many times. And then I repeated it to myself many times. I give these words to you. I know you need them. You take them and understand them and know their meaning in your own unique way. My interpretation was clear, as I heard him speak them, so I knew what he meant for me. To me, He meant that the transition from body to spirit was completely natural and easy. I also took this has he enjoyed the way it felt as he felt no pain when he passed. "It feels like when the wind blows!" I saw him grinning and chuckling, so I think he wants us to know that he's not suffering and that we shouldn't either. It's only a few words but sometimes all the answers we need are short and concise and simple. I hope you light up the bright part of your heart with this message. I truly believe your father's words are intended for exactly that.

Obviously I am in my own place of healing. I share this with you to help in any way. You can do the same, however you see fit. Aho mitake oyasin! With love.

7

Wombman

rom moment one we connected. So much so we both knew it and synchronistically acknowledged the energy between us. We didn't use words, it was just understood reading body language and just knowing exactly what information is presented. She opened her heart and world to me; she fearlessly allowed the moments to unfold in the stunning design that the universe created it.

Woman, I find, is so important to me. Names, she has many names. She gives and bleeds with me in a myriad of ways. Carly, Elizabeth, Claudia and others have filled in my life the roles of grace. How will they know me in future times, future worlds? They have filled the roles of friend, companion, confidante, lover, queen. Women in these forms can be called angels, for it's their nurturing and natural loving support that the human race needs to evolve spiritually and procreate the blossoming and brilliance of true unlimited God potential.

The opposite occurs as well. I've met many women

who have tapped into the power, the infinite side of themselves and egocentrically grown their identity and attached to it. They get a small taste of power, no different than that of men. In this taste of power, they have gotten their priorities misaligned and when they have children or give birth, they don't realize if their identity is focused on mortal body form instead of deity (which is the infinite part of themselves), the child will inherently feel this. The point is, it doesn't matter what kind of purse you have, the newest textiles, the newest spun silk, the most supple leather or whether your shoes have a brand name on them, or your car has the most popular badge. The women of this world can't get away with hiding behind their trends of fashion. Children need them to be the essence of the Goddess which is a feminine, nurturing, protective mother. She is a woman who values her own spiritual evolution in consciousness, a leader.

If you identify with these things, you must understand that your infant child feels the emotional vibration that you give yourself in this ego identity consciousness. They have no choice but to sponge this information in their, theta brain state. Their innocence feels your lack of attention and love for them as the center of your being. They feel how important your identity and new shoes are to you. The separation that they feel is really your separation and is no different than any other fall from grace. They are sweet and innocent precisely because they have not been fragmented by a fall from grace, so why as parents do you teach them to fall?

Whether it be ancient or current, the modern technological error; human reason will never be able to wrap itself around the infinite and spiritual part of themselves. So, we must return to wholeness not separateness. We must put our children at the center of our hearts in order to regenerate to the highest forms of human potential. Mother feminine, this is a role only you can fill.

I was instantly shocked by how well she (woman) read and worked with energy. Energy of the people around her and of the horses she took care of. See, we met at a spirited ranch in in the west, where the sun each day goes to die. I was so happy to have her invitation to come out and learn about horses, they had been obsessively on my mind for months. I knew I had to go be around them but was at a loss and had no one in my world to connect me with the ponies. I had been seeking and calling horse programs, calling out to their equine spirit. No one would allow me to pick their brains about horses, they were all too busy and why would they give a total stranger access to their private horses?

I only knew it was important for me emotionally to meet some horses, I didn't know why. When I contacted her, it could have gone either way, but she openly invited me out to meet her and her two horses. A shift occurred the moment we met. It's difficult to explain, it's a spiritual thing, a thing of new awareness. Her way, her connection is something unique and special. I knew she had perception into the finer realms of communication, I could sense it. It was lovely to be around her. I just didn't know if after the first day, if I could come back and learn more…yet.

Avoid gray areas.

There, the illusion of safety is guarded by the lies of "maybe," "sometime," and "I don't know." There is a truth. There is a way. Life is absolute, and its principles exacting. If you put it out there, it has to come back. Ask, and it must be revealed. Think, speak, and move with your desires, and nothing will ever be the same.

Those words she shared with me. She said the universe spoke them to her. I remember them and feel they are worth remembering.

It's a wonderful setting where Javier, a Mexican ranch hand tends to the horses. He feeds them, turns them out, looks after them, and assists in the births of new foals. He's a quiet and gentle soul who seems to be at ease with his world. I had been on horseback throughout my life many times and loved it. I felt energized and grounded in nature whenever I was in the presence of horses. They were big, strong and somewhat intimidating, still I was drawn to them and felt I had something to learn from them. Before I found this ranch, I spent months researching horses, healing, and horsemanship in my town. However, I found only dead ends as far as getting access to someone who would teach me about horses. I had thoughts of horses every day for months and for a while I thought it would pass, it would phase out.

One day I realized the urge to be around horses was intensifying as I could not stop thinking about them, though there was no specific reason for the obsession. Tired of no response to doors I knocked on, or people I contacted, I drove to an area near where I once lived in a tucked away town amongst the olive groves. I knew an address, and rolled up. Walking the grounds I found a worker, who led me eventually to the owner. I stated my interest but she said that her facility did not teach or offer horsemanship in the basic form. She thought a moment and gave the contact information of a woman she felt could help with my inquiries. I thanked her and soon after contacted her. Upon hearing her voice, I knew immediately she was happy and kind. I could hear it in her tone and expression. I stated my purpose, and she picked my brain for seriousness. After a short conversation she invited me out to her ranch where she had two horses and worked with other horses also.

I was so happy and felt myself looking forward to the few days later when I would meet her. When I landed at her ranch, I felt the land and its peace and I knew I was in a good place. She was standing in the barn and waved me over. We met, shook hands and smiled and she introduced me to her mare, a beautiful warmblood. Opening up, I shared my obsessive months of horses on the mind and said "I don't know why but I need to be around horses."

She understood, she knew exactly why and began to open her world and knowledge of the equine subtleties to me. This day was much more than I expected and I was so enthralled with her and her horses that I asked if I could come back sometime. She affirmatively said yes of course. The next few months of learning about and working with horses turned out to be one of the most prominent leaps in spiritual and emotional growth of my young life thus far. A heightened sense of awareness arises when a sacred horse lets you into to their trusting space and this allows a soulful primal form of communication to happen.

She let me into her world of horses and we knew in the first day that we liked each other and enjoyed our time together. She became more than a horse teacher to me; she became feminine loving soul, in many different aspects of companionship. We realized quickly that we both had an opportunity for heart growth if we just shared our authentic selves. She liked my mind and had never met a man in touch with his mind like myself. This is what she tells me. I know she functions from the heart and cares deeply, I learn to see it in the way she cares and loves her own self, it's beautiful.

Over time she speaks to me about emotion and spiritual concepts. She told me: "Realize you are a spirit here/now having a human experience. Once you truly know this, you can step back and observe from the witness perspective, you can observe from who you are, your spirit. Here you can choose to not get pulled into the drama of the physical senses and the physical body. Here you can live in a bit of meditation. You still know what's going on in your body, you just don't function from the emotionality or physiology of the body. An example is like when breathing through pain. You focus on breathing and you move through and become less identified with the pain."

She was able to heighten my ability to feel energy and tap into it. Up to this point I could only be aware of seeing energy and now I am at times able to feel it. The women in her taught me this.

She is intense, and she feels the world strongly. She can't help but communicate this to me when we are around each other. Sometimes I know she needs someone to release this with. I do my best, and she returns the favor when I need such things. Our hearts get intertwined and we converse like this;

I know things are processing for us both, and at times I find it hard to keep up. The navigation of uncharted terrain is so valuable; it offers us both a new energetic space in our hearts (spaces we have never felt before). It's not quite clear if we want the exact same things in this time but it is clear that we both love, honor, and cherish each other. This is to me, more important. I am writing this as a way of expressing and processing my feelings in this current moment. What the next moment brings, I know not. I only know that each moment knowing you is precious.

These words are of course my perspective and yours may be different. I want to share these words with you.

Our bond, was very unique, we were both engaged in openly assessing the bond itself, as it grew and changed, each day. It went something like this.

We are here for: learning the man/woman union on Earth and in spirit, to create, evolve, and nurture an energetic exchange of balance expansion and integrity.

Why I called you in: you offer a chance for me to be a better me and a better man. What higher gift could a woman give to a man than the ways, means, and encouragement to be a better man? You help me step into a deeper level of manhood. You are the true essence woman, the brilliance of the sacred feminine. I called you in to teach me about energetics, to see how to live a life tuning to energy, to heal myself, to bond, learn, and love the spirit of the horse, and to open grounding and heart chakras.

You've opened your world to me: your grace is astounding. The best word for it is grace. You are so sharing of your world, and a beautiful one it is. Your life experience as markers and references serves to stimulate my mind within a world. I intuitively wanted to know and now you've shown to me. How you are with people, horses, and relationships benchmarks a new way for me, a new awareness for me. What my soul knows it needs, you gladly give and share. I know it's healing and food for my soul. You feed my heart, what a gift you willingly give. I am so eternally grateful.

Helping me align with heart center: you've reminded me of starting from my heart, something I was doing before we met, but not consistently. Your way, your approach, your vision keeps reminding me simply by being in your presence to come from the heart. The more I see it in you, the more I can remember and practice it in me. I love being in your vibrational space, it's so heart centered and makes me know it's the true way to live a happy and fulfilling life, regardless of circumstances.

Love with honesty and integrity: your love, I feel! There is no doubt and this makes me feel so good and makes me want to love in return. It makes me a better man, a man of true fortitude not false pride. Your heart love shows me how to open with giving and receiving whilst being strong and real. The real vibration is so freeing, it tells me that love is honest, real, integrious, and renewing. To do this for me is what I need and crave as a human, your service in love expands me to levels I will never regress from. I can only vibrate this way from now on, whether with you or on my own.

Enabling me to be my authentic self and be honest with a woman: you've been so transparent and honest with me and asked the same from me, that offers me the chance to be not only my true self but my best self. Do you know how good that feels? Being honest with you, is to be honest with me, to step into my authentic self. It's like putting on the best pair of dusty boots that fit your inner self like a glove; the boots perfectly designed for the work your soul is meant to do. I am humbled and astonished by how hidden and afraid I've been in relationships before knowing you. I had not quite known how hidden I've been, I thought I was being true to myself and in most ways I was, but new light reveals where I fooled myself by coming from a fear state. This gift, I will always attribute and be ever grateful to you for showing me, and how to move in this way. You are such an incredible human, such a real woman; you are of rich fertile soil, brimful of life force. Truly awe inspiring!

Healing me: you have heart blasted me with your healing technique coupled with true intention of nurturing my well-being. Humans don't often do this for one another and you do it graciously. Your healing touch is so soothing, it takes me out of pain. This is the feeling I've been longing for my entire life. Having relief and movement out of pain is intensely mind blowing. It's like stopping a blizzard with the radiant warmth of the sun, I cannot truly explain the feeling it provides. I am just so thankful to you.

Teaching me energetics, forever shifting my perception: what a gift, do you realize what you've touched in me? You've taught me the perspective of what I've been feeling, but you've framed it with working tools and language to use and hone it. I see or should I say feel the world differently now. It's so much more real and connected for me. I can read relationships even better, And I know there is so much more to learn.

Another day is passed, and I find myself holding my head after a day's labor. Eyes are blind-sided with slumber. I miss the smell of the ranch, the horses. I nod my head from the kitchen table and choose to move toward my delicious bed, wrap myself up and release the tension of gravity, the bending of my light downward into my pillow. Asleep. Walking in the sun, moving east I walk with eyes half closed enjoying the cool slap of summer wind on my temples. I am near a ravine, along which I follow slightly downhill. It's dusty and crumbly near the precipice. Down, way down is a river, or water, like a large moving creek. A series of rocks appear to be neatly and perfectly placed and equally spaced in the center of the water. The one directly below is the biggest and is like a blob resembling a brain, it's craggy. Then six more cropping down the riverbed. The last one is so far away. It must be a mile or so and they are so evenly spaced apart, it's oddly symmetrical and their colors are not like ordinary rocks, the sparkle with flecks of mineral or bright dust. Such a sight to behold, I think to myself, how beautiful she is, Mother Nature!

I peer up, across the ravine, and there he is. He is there standing, holding his walking stick. I look directly at him, and he is still like a statue, like a tree, but there are no trees on that side of the ravine. I stare; he is perpendicular to me and not facing me. He must see me, but he doesn't move at all and his robe or cloak type thing does move in the breeze either. Instead stands and holding a stick in one hand and a cone-like stone in the other. The stone, or what looks like a stone from here, is black but slightly reflective in the light, it's speckled. What is he doing? The thought enters me. It's too far across to yell out, what is your name? A small vibration then comes up the cliff side as a wind, and a sound comes with it. "Thot, my name is Thot."

"What," I think in my head. Did I hear a thump in the wind that said Thot? I look down, then back up. He is a statue, as still as the mountains, miles behind him.

I stare at him, and then down into the ravine again, this process goes on for a while and once I looked down and focused on the shimmer of the water moving rapidly around the croppings of rocks. I began to be pulled closer to them. My awareness was drawn into an intimate and direct connection to the texture and location of the rocks. I was right on top of them. I focus on the second one, it was reddish. I could feel my visual perception move down next to the cropping and I could see it well. It was as if I was lying face down on top of it. I could see its grooves, and sharp edges, and its rough and edgy sparkles like specks of fool's gold in its mixture. My body was at the top of the ravine while my vision was intimately close to the shiny rock cropping, I was aware of both places at the same moment, and then I remembered Thot, and looked across the ravine to him. In a flash I was jolted into my head with a popping sound; I could see he was gone and realized I was no longer able to see the cropping below up close. I was limited again to the visual distance between myself and the bottom of the ravine. I sat for a few minutes and was quiet, then decided to walk along the precipice until I may find some direction. I walk, it was all pleasant, and I found myself replaying the memory of the rock cropping from the up-close perspective. As I did, I knew that when I was right on top of that rock, the water that rushed around it was moving incredibly slow, much too slow to be water, and yet is was certainly water. It looked and moved like water except it was in slow motion. In my mind it was mesmerizing to see the minute curves, splashes, and fractals go in and back unto itself. I was walking and not seeing where I was going, so when I realized this, I stopped replaying the vision in my head and started tracking my movements along the ravine.

Time when by, and I sat down to rest. I was still in my thoughts and I thought, where is Thot, and who is he, and I want to find him again. I hear a breath, slowly exhale from what sounds like right behind me. He is standing to my left, Thot is there immediately. I was startled but then relaxed and engaged in questioning him. Who are you? Where are you from? or what do you do?

He responded; "I, like you are here in this land as Thot but beyond it also. Here I have many names and here I resend the brightness of the sun to pull you and others into the vibration above this one. The sun is king and God is light, this is said and it is written in the ancient scriptures of Earth but you are here and not on Earth."

I said to him, "Yes I am on Earth, this is where I am and never have I been anywhere else."

He laughed and his eye started to glow. "You are not on Earth except when you go from spirit light into solid matter. You do this only when it is your turn to create an offering of consciousness to the Sun king. You are not on Earth, your mass is on Earth but you are here with me now and you are not your mass here, you are the dream under the light of the navel of the moon. You are like the divine degree of Celsius, fire is hot when next to ice and it is as cold as outer space when sitting next to the sun. Your relativity is by design, that of light. Your temperament and spirit is solid on Earth and liquid on Neptune and this temperature is powered by the sun. Without the sun your conscious life would not exist. You know all of this, remember. All life vibrations whether atomic, Plasma, man, animal, or mineral are such divinely powered as design by the light of the sun."

down, I feel it refreshing my throat and in my stomach. Intensely I realized I was dreaming and in stillness remember the words of temperature as I feel the room temperature water touching my inner esophagus. My mind goes back to Thot. I can see in my mind the rock in the ravine, and hear my own voice say to me…. *When a message is sent from heaven it is heard in the ravine while standing on each rock.*

I move on through my day, it's normal, fun, trivial. I go to bed at night and wake up in the morning and routinely go about work and the mundane. For weeks I am pondering the temperature of spirit and the ideas in my mind lead to read about Paracelsus. Paracelsus was an astrologer, physician, botanist, and alchemist from the fifteenth century. He discovered the elements hydrogen and nitrogen as well as founded the discipline of toxicology. He wrote about knowledge and light. He said that knowledge is obtained in two ways, by intuition and experience and that the purpose of intuition is present to the mind so new ideas, which to be realized, must be tested and proven by experience. These two processes are strengthening and developing each other. He said that the separation of these two will prove to be a disaster. These are linked to the right and left sides of the brain and also to that of feminine and masculine energies. This made me think of the grace and beauty of special women in my life. Right is intuition and left is experience. Intuition without experience allows the mind to fall into an abyss of speculation without adequate censorship by practical means. Experience without intuition could never be fruitful because fruitfulness comes not merely by the doing of things but from the overtones which stimulate creative thought.

According to Paracelsus, intuition is possible by the existence of a mysterious substance or essence, a universal life force. He called this force many things but primarily compared it to light. There are two kinds of light; there is the visible radiance which called brightness and the invisible radiance which he called darkness. There is no essential difference between the two. There is an invisible darkness that appears luminous to the soul but cannot be sensed by the body and there is a visible radiance which seems bright to the senses but may appear dark to the soul. He believed that light was the undeniable ground of all being, and that light not only provides the energy needed to support all creatures and the whole visible expanse of creation but the invisible part of light supports the secret powers and functions of man, particularly intuition. Intuition therefore relates to the capacity for the individual to become attuned to the hidden side of life.

By light then, Paracelsus implies much more than the radiance of the sun, a lantern, or a candle. To him light is the perfect symbol or emblem or figure of total well-being. Light is the cause of health, and invisible light, no less real if unseen, is the cause of wisdom. As the light of the body gives strength and energy sustaining growth and development, so the light of the soul bestows understanding. The light of the mind makes wisdom possible, and the light of the spirit confers truth. Therefore truth, wisdom, understanding, and health are all manifestations or revelations of one virtue or power. "What health is to the body, morality is to the emotions, virtue to the soul, wisdom to the mind, and reality to the spirit". (Paracelsus)

I realized Paracelsus was holistically syncing our humanness to light; the emanations of our composition, the four rivers; solid, liquid, gas, and radiance. This shot me into a remembering of something Thot spoke to me while walking through a silted creekbed. He started to elaborate on a tribe of West Africans, who he said either parted from or gave rise to the pre-dynastic magi of ancient Egypt. He asked me if I knew about them, the Dogon people? I replied, of course not, why? He went into their old, old ways of profound knowledge and seeing the universe, then recording it in symbol and cosmology. He said they created a shaman hood order to initiate others. Those who are persistent in asking the right questions are initiated over time to higher truth. There was a system kept in the body and mind of shamans that encouraged education, apophatic thinking, and a genuine desire to know. They taught with nature and cosmology the structure of matter, procreation, regeneration, and genetics of the first humans. They developed symbols with deep layers of sacred scientific meaning about the universe and their place within it. They knew that all science was based on metaphysical and esoteric principles and without these elementals, science was fruitless and lacked in emotion and meaning. All science is revealing the universe so it must sync religion, theology, philosophy, art and consciousness into a unified whole. If it did not, its relevance and truth would be trivial and short lived.

Also, he said, the Dogon (People of western Egypt) embodied equality and so shunned heredity and hierarchy of knowledge. When empiricism usurps control over knowledge it is doomed to destroy itself because it has lost sight of truth and so corrupts or distorts knowledge. They knew humans were dual (split into male and female) and so encoded dual sides of scientific concepts of each symbol. Thot said, for example the city of Heliopolis was paired with the city Thermopolis and each city held one side of the symbols of knowledge. Heliopolis represented the structure of matter and the way light waves travel and manifest creation. Thermopolis represented genetics and reproduction so mitosis, chromosomes, zygotes, and embryonic growth. God or the cell (wholeness) is said to form out of water to divide itself into the perfect dualist pair (the vesica pisces), to form man who must find balance as he is both male and female energies. Four original males and four original females systematically mated to spawn all humans and sustain the cycle with diversity. He then said, in time you will deeply understand these symbols, and I will show them to you someday. It becomes clear that they give rise to modern cosmologies like the story of Adam and Eve, and many others.

He goes further to tie into our four elemental vibratory states or bodies. All humans have a physical body (senses) and the remaining three bodies (spirit, mind, emotion) have their vibratory and atomic signatures in light. These are known as platonic solids. We are light rays, we are powered and energized by light and on Earth by the sun. This is why all ancient and lasting spiritual cultures attuned and worship the sun, even if they had to do it in secrecy. Radiation of light is positively charged and gravitation is negatively charged. Radiation voids matter. This is expressed when the soul leaves the body and ascends. While gravitation contracts and produces matter (bending light), the soul descends with electricity into the body into the embryo. Light in essence is not only physical, it is psycho-spiritual.

The light of the physical sun warms and reveals the bodies of things. The light of the psychic sun nourishes and reveals the structure of the soul. The light of the spiritual sun sustains and nourishes the human spirit. The sun is birthing the trinity in our solar system; it is a three aspect body of physic, psychic, and spirit.

Pythagoras also describes light as spirit. He states, "a deity is an infinite being whose body is composed of the substance of light and whose soul is composed of the substance of truth. Truth is therefore a kind of light and when it shines, a kind of darkness is dissipated. Truth is to the darkness of ignorance what the physical sun is to the darkness of nature. There is also a spiritual sun and the total energy of this sun dissipates total illusion that is morality or materiality. The spiritual sun is forever dispelling the kind of darkness which we call death. The psychic sun is forever dissipating the kind of darkness which we call ignorance. And the physical sun is forever dissipating crystallization". (Pythagoras).

Much of modern science is fragmented and inefficient due to it consistently relying on the effects present in nature. The effects we sense are only palpable within the senses and so mapping the effects, may increase man's ability to reason, yet have no knowledge within of the cause of these effects. It would be like attempting to hear music by looking through a microscope. These effects, although vibrations of light, are in the realm of effects and thus sensed by the sense organs only. The realm of truth and knowledge lie hidden beyond the left brain of the intellect and can only be accessed directly in the right brain of intuition. This delineates the difference between thinking and knowing.

A life of constant thinking offers a loop of stress that is harmful to the body, mind, and soul of the human and creates deficiencies, disease, and imbalances. If one opposes this viewpoint, rest assured they are functioning from the fragmentary realm of the intellect only. If they bridge the gap of the two hemispheres and join the left and right sides, the flood of consciousness, by design, begins to know knowledge holistically. The illusion of effects can be detected and measured for certain, however the movement of these effects is still an illusion. Universal mind thinking bridges to cosmic consciousness and knowing is available to all elemental bodies of the human being. The light is the truth and the truth shall set you free. Tuning into the causal is where knowledge resides, and the intellect, no matter how clever, cannot harmonize or integrate this action.

I hear the distinct voice of Thot from time to time. He intuitively knows exactly when to chime in. As I sit in meditation of new concepts, I hear his voice. He says short cryptic messages that prompt visualizations and generate a narrative in my mind. Continuing until one image completes its story message, and then he delivers another. He begins talking about Egypt and says one of the biggest fallacies in your time is that your people are taught that your time is the most advanced in human history. You people so vainly think that there was no science or technology in olden times and so you preposterously assume there were no geniuses among your ancestors.

I began to see a story of images unfold. We think our culture has it all aligned in categorical boxes and that the history we are taught in school is perfectly valid. So untrue. Why are we taught not to question? Don't you see the greatest minds of our heroes are exemplary and are so brilliant precisely because they did question their societies postulates!

Thot said, "remember when you stood on the rock cropping, when in the ravine? Those rocks are the messengers of the heavens. What the stars are up there, tells you what the chakras are down here. The Earth is the material microcosm of the heavens. This is why old sages and lovers of wisdom call the highest thinking cosmic consciousness, it is boldly cosmic, and you are it. The seven rock croppings are the Earth's energy centers and when you stand on them you balance and charge your own. The energy flows upward through the spine to the seat of the soul, the pineal gland. The river in the ravine is the spinal fluid, and the river delta is the higher brain.

The human history is written by him, the conquerors of men, so he calls it *his-story*, and you believe it, in vain. Vibrate your awareness to go inward and shifts in reality occur, your being expands. You must go in in order to expand; it is a grand paradox of polarity. In Egypt your history has been tampered with by a ruling elite group of men. They think themselves superior to others and are so maniacal, they willingly pervert the symbols and history of sacred knowledge that was built and preserved for the benefit of all humans equally. They feel they are not your equal, but your superior, so they sell you an alternate version of reality, be known this is in the time you are born in. They are of a selfish and paranoid mind and thus will never ascend to the high creator.

The early dynasties of the Nile region were of good character and the king's goal in life was the same as is in his death, to go to the stars from which human origins began. There is a piece of dust in all humans that started in the beginning of creation. This dust transforms through cosmic creation itself to one-day birth the Earth and its people. The noble kings knew this and lived a life of sacred honor to this process, this miracle of life. Through Earth catastrophe, the minds of men were coerced into fear by a group that think themselves as royal elite. They became psychopaths and purchased power by selling to people the idea that they can stand in for God (the higher mind). Once people agreed, they lost their own power. They lost their ability to respond, they lost their own responsibility.

Ever since, people have elected men to interpret cosmic consciousness for them. They have elected the vicar, one who stands in for God. The vicar gladly takes on the role and mocks you as he/she sells you your thoughts and education…for a price…for profit.

You are still sold this today. For example, you read that ancient Egypt was a primitive society, and you believed this simply because you have today's science and a television. With intuitive reason, you soon realized this cannot be true. Do understand that there have always been intelligent humans and geniuses in all times and in all cultures. These geniuses built architectural feats still unattainable today. They mapped the precession cycles of the stars for thousands of years; they built alphabets and languages out of numbers that you still use today. The basis of what they did, gave rise to your civilization in this modern time. They quarried seventy ton pillars of granite from over six hundred miles away and erected them fifty meters high (without even a scratch) within the great pyramid. They carved the base stones of the temple of Jupiter at Baalbek and moved them into place. These stones are over six hundred thousand tons. Why would they do this? Why would they go to such great lengths? Because they were geniuses tapped into the sacred and they wanted future humans to know their own divinity as well. Don't forget, the sun enables this all!

As these ancients used their creativity and intuition, they use the technology of the time to do these things. They used the process of internalization to find and uncover the laws of truth and nature. In many ways they are much closer to the truth than modern man. To these ancients, their beginnings start with the God Osiris and he was from the Orion nebula star system. Later kings built pyramids for multiple reasons but the primary one was to return to the throne of the stars where Osiris dwells. The purpose for the great pyramids of Giza is still a mystery to your modern man, why? Because you are not internalizing your geniuses or your sacred. The great pyramid has no writing in it describing its purpose, think about that. Builders didn't put their names on it or its meaning. They want you to discover it for yourself. They were not vain and seek no notoriety; they want to share sacred knowledge with those who have eyes to see and ears to hear.

Almost all other pyramids in the Nile region are filled with writing, which are now known as the pyramid texts. They tell us much about the minds and ambitions of those people but the great pyramid is more precise and purposeful. It is not a tomb, as there have never been any mummies found there, it marks the movement of certain stars. It aligns with Orion's belt, it is a mapping of this constellation in time and the sphinx is much, much older so it was built before the great pyramid, which tells you they knew about cathedral thinking. Cathedral thinking is likened to the depth of planning and foresight required to build a lasting cathedral that resonates generations into the future. It's an approach that ties in a massive amount of insight and details and few people have the ability to employ it successfully. They planned this hundreds of years in advance. The sphinx is looking at the constellation leo as it rises in the south, so if you reverse engineer this, you find it was built when it aligned perfectly, which was 12,500 BCE. The sphinx and the pyramid both mark constellations in the eastern sky and their pathways from the Nile aligning with the summer and winter solstice, this is why the pathways are angled slightly.

So I tell you these things, and knowledge is given. As for forming a belief, understand that believing is caught in the mind and knowing is caught in the heart. Question every belief you have and see which ones are truly serving you, and then you will eventually come to knowing. We uphold our reality with our word, our internal dialogue. As it is said, in the beginning was the word, and the word was God. The ancients lived more in tune with the cosmic cycles and thus the natural world. They practiced meditation, which is the stopping of the internal dialogue, stopping the incessant chatter of the mind. When we stop the internal dialogue we reveal where the body and the mind are incongruent. We uphold and create reality with our inner dialogue so if our talk is not aligned with our body (what we are doing), then we are fragmented. If they are in line then we manifest reality with ease, and there is union. Living in union is the key to transcendence and wholeness, which is happiness. The ancients, who you've been taught didn't even have the wheel, knew this and they lived more in accordance to union and wholeness. They were of genius mind, universal mind.

When a message from the heavens is heard, it is first heard in Heliopolis (the heart), repeated at Memphis and then Thermopolis where it is written. Then it is heard in the great city of Thebes. These rock croppings/cities are the chakras of earth from the heart to the head, along the spine of the great Nile River." He went on to say, "listen closely to the wisdom of old...Spirit is the ambition that motivated those Egyptians to place those magnificent stones where they lay now and give you a blessing of knowledge millenniums old. Don't discount them with your modern atonist education of materialism. Atonism is a self-serving controlling mentality that can lead to psychopathy. Spirit is infinite living mind and being man, nothing can rise higher than its source and man was made of creator source. Man is the image of God only by degree, the degree of matter.

Only when man becomes a higher degree, does he

become infinite living mind. He needs to attain the whereabouts and then unity of his counterpoint, some call this the twin soul. It is a maneuver of the most paramount unity of being. Truth is always of debate, due to each person's perspective of unique reality. So both sides of truth are always true. One is relative and the other absolute. Every pole has its dual, its desired opposite. Using the will, change your vibration to your desired state. Mind, metals, and elements can be transmuted from state to state and degree to degree. Transmute the fragmented mind into infinite mind, the mind of cosmic consciousness, the mind of union. This is practiced and achieved, as mental alchemy. Hermes said, he who sees that nothing rests and that everything is vibration, grasps the scepter of power. Seeing the conflict between truth and lies, he sees the story, the truth in you, the truth in the universe, he sees his own divinity. This is why a fragmented mind can only lead to unhappiness. Ancient wisdom is here because it's old; it's still here because it's relevant. The mystic, shaman, nagual is so dynamic, elusive, mesmerizing for one reason alone…He is mystical because he has direct access to truth.

She came back into my head, woman, her name is unimportant. I sensed the soul in her. She was Mesmerizing. I was listening to Thot and my attention was vibrating to stay focused on his descriptions when she flooded into to my mind. I drifted away with her and he paused and wriggled his chin a bit. I sensed the indescribable feeling of my face softly caressing her cheeks.

He pointed his elbow gently at me and said, "don't think you're special, don't be too self-important." He said, "all of us feel this frustration, it is the second split and it's brutal but necessary. The split of gender is found throughout the cosmos and became a principle of universal law by the great creative architect."

I couldn't follow his words. I was lost in her nuances, her smoothness, feelings only given by woman.

He said, "You feel it deep in your bones because you were born into chaos and competition, this causes constant tension. Competition makes you show and prove your worth because your split and you feel that you are in lack. This is the remembering to stalk and find your counter point or twin soul, the female part to your male soul. A great insecurity is dissolved when we find and unite with our second split and when this occurs we realize we are never in a state of lack. We are never in lack because the great spirit, by its inner nature, always through virtue, provides."

I felt a warm feeling in my throat and chest, like crying but in an endearing way, like being happy that you're melancholy because it's somehow worth it.

He said, "all of us are split by gender and we are attracted to the opposing sex to regenerate both physically and spiritually, this includes the emotions and the mind. We all move through the matrix of being, searching for our original gender split, we remember this part of us when we see it because it is our reflective counter point of light within the soul. We may meet many people with similar vibrations which remind us who we originally are but once united within our soul in harmonic gender we resonate as whole and spin from within, higher and higher.

Each divine ego or soul is a still point of light, a sun enfolded. The male sun is inclined to self-realization in terms of wisdom and knowledge of creation while each female sun is inclined to realize beauty and divine love. Each soul needs the other, the still point in the other to realize their higher states in each other and then unite them."

As I transform through this weighty knowledge, I open my heart to send living thanks to the sacred women in my life. I acknowledge the intimate connection these people have shared with me and I know I would not be a man without them. This state of union is the divine yoga and cosmic consciousness cannot be attained without it. The split was done to birth manifestations of the universe, it's light or consciousness birthing itself over and over. Man in this state realizes the unification to her (woman) womb-man which is all of creation, she is birth cosmic and eternity. This is krst, christ, krishna, crystalline, consciousness of her sacred feminine. The union with the active infinite, the great spirit.

As he told me this, I began to love her. She was not present, but I felt such grace and honor for her, the woman. She is lost without man and just as he is destitute without her. She in her honesty became the gift of honesty I could finally see in myself. In that moment I exploded with gratitude and I spoke within to her in my heart as I knew there is no greater gift a person can give to another than that she gives to me. Love.

8

ANTIONETTE

God never engages in phenomenon for the sake of phenomena. There is a purpose and a design to everything. She sees that there may be a Teacher in the light, it is possibly Saint-Germain who I see in the light. He is someone who has aided me in other life times. There is a (John) and (William) that is on the other side and has been trying to help me. I have and she says I have ability to develop clairvoyance. God has shown me this in the light. She says I should work with the energy and always put white light around me use it as a guide to make decisions. She says Uncle Mike has come through for musical support, she first said this in 1997, he loves me. Antoinette herself, she lives by Edgar Cayce's medical advice, she was down to 89 pounds and thought she was dying when she first found out she has scleroderma. She lived, and that's how she met John Lawrence. John Lawrence told her she was spared by the God force. She was given gifts of clairvoyance. She was never to do a public show of her gifts.

God trusts her to never get into the way of his agenda and to keep the ego out of the gift. She tells me that I am to learn about meditation, it will serve me. She says astral projection does not bring deeper spiritual awareness, it is a phenomenon. Meditation enhances the light body, providing an ever increasing awareness. Energetic shifts are the work of the true medicine man and they affect the emotional awareness of a problem so as to see the healing emotional space to be in. Thus the body and the mind heal.

My time, each minute with Antoinette is special. I feel so fortunate to have her in my life, a friend of a thousand years, a soul genuine in the intent to help and love those around her. I don't know if other people have met or know holy persons, but I am blessed to have her in my life. I also feel I should not neglect her or take her for granted, I know all things of matter are temporal and will someday disappear. I prod her with questions when I can, I must be wise to tap into her wisdom and yogic knowledge. After this session with her, I began to recharge and study more on my own. I began digging into ancient texts and philosophers.

I began to piece together ideas and form them for myself. From the awake state of the psyche, one slowly learns that only an individual can awaken and shake himself from sleep. When this begins to occur; they most certainly feel a desire to wake others, but this is not so. Others must intend to wake themselves and maybe through vibration each will recognize their own volition and desire to be. The collective Jungian mind is organic and will awaken of its own accord. The breeze of that day will whisk away the lightest of blossoms into the heights of the warm blue skies.

According to Plato, to find the maker and father of this univer selfhood by being it within (embodiment). They offer no revelations themselves but are the conduit that the great spirit flows through. It sees fit to do so. They say, don't follow me, don't take my word for it. Be still and stand in the light of the sun and you yourself will see your own awakening. I began to realize that the truly wise and enlightened never promise the gift of salvation, because they know by experience that no one gave it to them and they may not give to another. It is only achieved by attuning your light, the lamp within to the light of infinite consciousness and getting out of your own way, then allowing yourself to give it to yourself. Deep within this cosmic principle is the deepest of knowledge; as the ancient druids kept sacred the words, you are your own shaman. In you claiming your divine rite, bow to no man and serve everyone. The issue here is most souls are not ready to handle the rumblings of this vibratory state, they're not willing to come out of slumber and be conscious of the power and potentiality that the divine human can hold. They would much rather be the creature of comfort and play hide and seek with themselves. This is because the truth is an incredibly powerful and mystical current that moves all creation. The cosmic laws still apply and the highest chakra is always polarized and reflected in the lowest, its yin/yang. As above so below; as within so without. This principle applies also to human thinking. If you are the atheist in your highest cosmic thoughts, then dwelling in self-denial in your lowest. If you are fearful, vain, and deny the existence of a universal source and sustainer without wielding such power yourself, then you are feeding the ego of intellect and manifesting your own psyche of spiritual dyslexia. If you are a tyrant in your thoughts then in your body you become a slave.

It is such a treacherous slope to traverse and like viewing a drawing of depth, height, volume, and density and being aware of the flatness of the image only. The four dimensions are aligned in the paper of two dimensions, but remain flat and locked into the twofold world but the four-fold world exists there in mind if you could only be in the genius mind of the architect holding the pen, you would see.

Awareness, is so peculiar as it exists and maneuvers itself on all points in all dimensions, simultaneously. But you can only be locked into the awareness of all points if you give yourself the potential to do so. The ground of being offers you the ability to commune with it from one limited point of vantage or all of them, from the still cause to the infinite. Only the fearful and quivering deny themselves this blessing. And the greatest of human minds, hold out the lantern and from the deep lungs howl out to them, WAKE UP.

The divine ego, so difficult! It's hard to believe, hard to know if it's real, and hard to know if it's lying. In so, it secretly and consistently reveals division and this is how you know its motive. If you deem yourself the physical sense and the body only, then your consciousness will be just that. Conversely if you expand your thoughts to be all of that and the spirit animating your being, then your consciousness will be just that. This is the nature of consciousness, it is itself deeply enfolded and will be aware of whatever level of unfolding attained. Light is the same, matter and the physical body are light enfolded into density.

Ego is not a bad thing. It is self in a shallow survival center and reflects a small light upon the vast ocean of consciousness. The narcissist is the ego who loathes themselves. This shallow lamp reflects the inauthentic self, known as the mortal body. The vast ocean of consciousness is the source of being itself and reflects all light of infinite consciousness. It is boundless and undivided.

I keep coming to the conclusion that the issue in all relationships (physical and metaphysical) is union. Once you see the body is the temple of God, you must, must respond. When looking to the stars do you see separations or one vast infinite body? When you look within do you see separate cells fighting? When you look in your mind do you see separate emotions, egos, and intellects or do you see all of infinite consciousness? When daylight shines to your awareness, it doesn't shine from up there and hit you, it shines from up there and is you. When night fall arrives it doesn't dimly hit you. It arrives from up there and is you. It is light shining in an unconscious state; it is the spectrum of sleeping light.

Everything has a spirit (a non-physical counterpart). Any material body is moved by a non-physical counterpart called energy (spirit). When you ingest an animal or drink a plant you are ingesting another consciousness, you are energy transforming another energy. You are ingesting their intelligence and spirit and you merge to create a new consciousness. Man being self-conscious, clearly has his spirit. You can see it reflected in his eyes and in his heat. If man has his spirit, so does the infinite cosmos have its spirit. Deep within unity consciousness merge into it.

I began to see, unity all around me then saw its source within me. Look at the ancient culture all around the world, so many have the serpent as their symbol. Look deep and see the unity of the serpent's division. He being the wave manifestation of light; moves as a snake moves. He cracks the cosmic egg in the form of the male sperm, to bring regeneration through electric force. The egg or female receives through her magnetic and toroidal force. The serpent is always the bringer of knowledge and rests in the tree of knowledge. He reveals symbolically two trees, one of everlasting life and one of sure death.

But look deeper, see they are but one tree polarized and differentiated into the illusion of two. Like the man and the woman, the head and the feet, the heart and the brain. Still-light divided, gives birth to the alpha and the omega, the beginning and the end, the yin and the yang, the light and the darkness. In the sight of union, we see clearly the waveform of the serpent is not the cast out heathen, he is the messenger of knowledge and shunned for his purpose because knowledge can be offensive, but not a sin. In the highest knowledge of truth is freedom.

My time with Antoinette is always marked by light pulsations, and shifting perceptions. Some of the new shifts happen when in her presence, in those precious moments we are in each other's company. Other shifts happen later as a result of the light flowing through her. She came into my life when I was nineteen years old. A very strange circumstance placed me on her doorstep. I was led there by the great spirit only I couldn't know that until later in life. She is the nagual (the incarnation of the infinite) for me. Although she would probably call herself a yogi, which she is. She shared teachings of Kriya yoga with me, which still guide me today. Who is she? A loving mystery. The masters of light surround her and appear through her to be messengers of the most high. Somehow these great masters know her and commune with her and serve as healing medicine for myself and others. She forever marks my life as the great shift into the engagement of awakening for me. After knowing her, I am forever changed. After a recent meeting with Antoinette, I dove deeper into my studies of the mystery schools of the ancients, primarily the Abrahamic occult. Thot appeared in my tiny yellow kingdom, my chamber abode. He came to speak guiding messages of short but potent guide posts from which I should start my studies.

On this particular day, I was deep into the serpent culture and the serpent symbols around the world. In hidden sources I will not reveal, the dot further connected and the unification of the serpent in the west became clear. The serpent is the kundalini energy of the Hindus, coursing naturally up and down the human spine. It is healing and the procreative life force itself and is regulated like the planet by our sun. In the book of genesis, woman (womb-man linked to death and birth) is the messenger of the words of the serpent; she is a secondary symbol of the serpent as she carries the knowledge of birth. The story goes that we are not to eat of the tree of knowledge (of right and wrong) or we shall die. This is the allegorical death of spiritually dying and refers to a shift in self-awareness, the awareness of our own death. A powerful concept to behold for any sentient being. The serpent says to her, you will not surely die for God knows that the day you eat of it your eyes will be open and you will be like God, knowing good and evil. As God the creator of all, he/she knows both good and evil because he/she created them. The unaware, naive to higher spiritual consciousness have no knowledge of their own death, they don't know they have a self, so function solely on instinct. See, the tree of knowledge (of good and evil) will make you like God because when you eat of that which is within (the self) you become responsible for your thoughts, reality, and actions; you become self-realized. God being the creator, is self-renewing and eternally self-sustaining, never dependant on any outside force. There is no outside force, SEE. When you become a self-realized sovereign master, all of your creation is yours, both good and bad you are self-empowered as man the procreator.

When man was cast outside of the garden or paradise (para means close to and *dise* or *deis* means god) he became ignorant of his higher nature, his creative center. He must have done so, by refusing to be attentive and responsibly aware of his balancing of good and evil, he began to fear himself instead of love himself. He became afraid of his own creative power, he fragmented and his subtle energetic body became more dense, and earthly. The garden is the paradise center of divine self, outside that is the lower nature. In gnostic, Egyptian, syncretism, essene, and shemsu hor teachings, Eve (keeping things even) is symbolically always close to the serpent knowledge, as she is the keeper and protector of this sacred knowledge, the fire within, the life force of sexual union and birth. It makes so much sense.

As writing developed out of symbol; so did politics controlling it and its meanings. Certain groups misused and demonstrated (strata of the demon) the knowledge to suit their own sinister agenda, thus perpetuating man's further fall away from himself. Modern churches and interpretations of the scriptures are almost always perverted, as even the church leaders have no knowledge of their own system origins or history. The misled are misleading the misled. This is why Eve is portrayed so badly in Abrahamic religion, they did this to control and educate the peasants for their mental enslavement and manipulation.

"Nature is the self, your entire idea about yourself is borrowed, from those who have no idea who they are" Osho

Man can, will, and must involve to evolve himself out of his self-induced fear of knowing right from wrong. He must unhide from fear to stop seeing reality being run from his inner tyrant. In this same way Antoinette teaches the truth that we must learn symbol literacy and esoterics on syncretism and number in order to return to nature. Humans must balance male/female polarity in all four bodies to keep the serpent kundalini spinning healthily and harmoniously. See the symbol of Abraxis, man holding and balancing two serpents. Hold the power of the serpent in your hand and the force that sustains all being is in your palm to marvel at but it is not yours to own, it cannot be possessed and has no ego or identity, because as we have seen, it is universal.

So through the natural order of things, knowledge is transmitted to conscious man through the process of mediumship. All forces and dimensions move themselves and their knowledge through the enfolding process of consciousness. The elements here on Earth speak to us; we just have to learn to listen. We detect our science through the elementals and they as fire, air, earth, and water are spiritual mediums of the natural order. The elementals are by design messengers of truth, and they reveal to the sensitive mind. They cannot deceive.

"The id, like the mind is not a thing or a place. It has not material circuitry, it is simply a way of seeing, an act of perception. Man, by perceiving or seeing, the nature around him and more importantly within him, nucleate opposites. The body itself, the being itself is the temple of the miraculous. The action of observing an object immediately objectifies it. The seer, being the center self, or center of consciousness nucleate the object of observation. Perception itself unifies subject and object. Man himself is the unity consciousness, if he so learns how to see." - Thomas Saaze

To all that are closed and in disbelief, I say man (embodied spirit), has knowledge available to him, always, each moment, at his fingertips. The order of things says he may know it only by being willing to unlearn his current belief systems. Pause here to inventory your reaction and then suspend your current belief system, even for a moment. Stalk your inner believer as the great Toltecs do and ask: where is my beliefs origin? Who or what cult first gave it to me, where and when did it arise? At man's grasp is this intrinsic knowledge, as Socrates so eloquently said "the greatest evil is ignorance, and the greatest good is knowledge".

One way to grasp this knowledge is by understanding the way it's transmitted to us. Through the process of mediumship, knowledge comes to us. It waxes and wanes like dusk and twilight through the ages/yugas of gold, silver, bronze, and iron. Even with its variations upon consciousness, it is always here, enfolded within being itself, enfolded within matter itself. We have just to apply our sincere intent to call it out of us. It transmits and receives on all depths and dimensions through mediumship. Please see the great works of Thomas H. Burgoyne to study this deeper. From infinity, down to man, then to the mineral are all the descending levels of mediumship and we are receiving it in the densest level, this is why we are easily forgetful of our spiritual counterpart. The higher mind dispenses to the lower mind and the higher mind is influenced by yet even higher spheres. The knowledge is spiraling down even if we are unconscious of it, and reveals itself in the very basic order of as above, so below.

I began, like many, to ask myself how can everything be enfolded within everything? But it appears to be so. The atom is packed with even smaller particles and they surrounded by oceans of space, space infused with intelligent energy. At every level we see chasms within cosmos, micro within macro edifying the principle of the wisest earth mind Hern/Thoth/Hermes. Herne, Thoth, and Hermes are all the same being. He is the cosmic principle who weighs your heart in balance with a feather to see how much light and love you've created within. This ceremony is that of graduation from initiation. If a pure heart is found, the beyond is open to you. So once you pause and suspend your current conditioning and beliefs, you immediately make room for deeper levels of enfolded knowledge to reveal itself to you. As light moves (regenerates itself immaculately) it does so in ordered spirals or vortices. It is nature's movement.

In expansion/explosion it wastes energy to constantly overcome resistance while in implosion there is no resistance. The enfoldment pattern itself negates any resistance and so it creates and harvests energy. Protons are stretched, even though they are round bodies, away from equilibrium (180 degrees from each other) toward the crest of solstice. This is how a moving round body stretches into a waveform. If such a body be only pulled in one direction, it becomes a linear line of light but if stretched in two directions simultaneously it bends into crests and troughs of the undulation wave form. And the most ancient of symbols, the cross (+) is but the crests of solstices and equinoxes moving through levels of enfolded densities.

On to the body, the light waves hit and penetrate and power the body's own inner light to fold. In the esoteric teaching, breath be implosion and explosion, thus with the bodies first breath is the correspondence and polarization of the heavenly planets at that moment. We birth and live interconnected to the cosmic macrocosm reflecting in our natal temple called our body. Understand that these astrological planets don't rule our being, they inform and mold it to the extent of our awareness of their natural movements and principles. Every man has the power to awaken and know himself and consciously turn his vices into virtues. As Burgoyne says, "deep within the breath lies the rhythm of cosmic light which lives within the human heart. The web of light ruled by the moon ensnares the soul to the earth body but deep in the silence of the heart lies the light of the still causal God which when accessed will break the ensnaring web, giving way to the awareness of cosmic infinity. This frees the soul from the illusion of matter and the body. Breath being the medium of the fractal of immortal spirit into the patterns of matter, ever changing, each moment".

I segue a bit here to integrate the mystical works of Rudolf Steiner. As I study him, I see I must revisit his words to grasp the meanings of his syntax. The Egyptian mysteries, he clearly links to the Brahman teachings of India. So with the light enfolded human form, it goes as such.

Since we are made of light, our source of light, are the celestial spheres. For example, Moon and Sun. As stated, the human body being the temple of God is enfolded and encoded in the harmonics of scientific light and sound. These forces harmonize in form, all manifestation, the human body being among the most brilliant. Its brilliance lies in both its annihilation of the physical manifestation, and the simultaneous immortal consciousness of spirit. I must say, in a little tangent, that the idea of extraterrestrials, manipulating man as if an in experiment, is not only incorrect but short sighted. We must see, that although life exists in other spheres of the universe, it does not enter the earth through metallic spacecraft and fly between planets. This is a narrow view of the way in which light, life manifests. The point is, yes there are higher beings or entities which communicate, and affect mankind. However, man is a sovereign being, man's potential to claim it, in his own mind body and soul are given to him thus he needs no extraterritorial force, in order to be a whole being himself. Moving on to the way in which Sun and Moon affect and manifest the human body through the Osiris and Isis mythology.

First, with the works of Rudolf Steiner, and his mystical clairvoyance, we see that the human essence has been an evolutionary process connected to the earth. Meaning, that when gaseous light nebula that was Earth, Moon, and Sun all together in one cloud, before full physical manifestation, the human being in its spirit was there present. Just not in the same form as he is refined today. As these bodies become more dense, they moved away from each other. But as we can see, the Earth, Moon, and Sun although separate from each other are still moving and communicating in harmony which is interdependent. Once we see their interconnectedness, we can understand the stories of these cosmic principles given names such as Osiris, who was the Sun principal, and Isis, who was the moon principle.

Although most people will find this hard to fathom, the human body truly designed by light, has manifested its shape and organs based on the movements of planetary and luminous bodies. In order for man to be fully physical, a spinal cord with sensitive nerve filaments must have developed. A tree of life planted in the body, one sensitive to the cosmos. And so it did, and this we call the cosmic principle of the union between Osiris and Isis, the male/female. So for men to be whole sovereign beings who claim their own power, and their own conscious awareness, a body needed, in such a way to be formed.

The point is, the harmonics of the moon, its 14 day influences are said in the myths to be the body of Osiris. The body of Osiris is originally the Sun and solar light, so we must see that the moon is reflecting the solar consciousness of Osiris. The story goes, that Osiris split himself into duality, giving birth to his brother set who is also known as Typhon. We get the cosmic principle of the winds of change known as the typhoon from this word and name. These 14 nerve filaments correspond directly to the phases of the Moon. However, the 14 phases of the Moon are doubled, they have different aspects from New Moon to full moon, and different from full moon back to new moon. Thus we have 28 phases, this is the regulation of the human body in forms of water and salt, also this is why the female human, is regulated in her menstrual cycle to roughly 28 days.

So the human, being both male and female energies, have 14 days of Osiris influence, and 14 days of Isis influence. Each human is both male and female, in their etheric bodies. And since the lunar year and solar year do not timeout the same, the development of further nerve filaments which make up the entire spine came to be. It is important to realize that man's form, is not rigid in the system, it is an evolutionary form of manifested consciousness. So, man's physical form influenced by the moon, hardens the body, and is balanced out by the Sun which makes the body elastic. This process is ongoing, as man's form is evolving into more refined forms.

As the story goes, Osiris was originally one whole being, Set or Typhon, his jealous brother, killed him and cut him into 14 pieces and then buried him in the sea. Isis, his wife lovingly uncovered all the pieces and then put his body back together. However, the process of being put back together makes him a new aspect; so man's body reflects the idea of unity being divided and then put back together into a sovereign whole. This abstract concept goes further into more refined bodily roles. In ancient Egypt, the lungs were a symbol of the winged solar disk. Following this line, we see that man's consciousness is regulated through breathing, and the process of the breath being the universe inhaled into the physical body, is what Set caused to Osiris. The opposing forces of duality constantly spinning evolve each moment into new refined forms of consciousness. And so the lungs, being twins, and also having both male and female energies, are the cause of man's bodily temple to remain conscious with each breath. All forms in the universe are always striving toward unification.

It is the beauty of light manifested from the cosmos, and also in the microcosm of the human being form. Through this balance of male female aspects, the Sun and Moon power that the human body still to this day, is regulating fertility and procreation. And so is Isis and Isis made a son, in the name of Horus. This crystal consciousness of Horus, is the icon of solar deity birth on earth, and so man typically worships this archetype as his higher self. The consciousness of balance and harmony and love.

Each time I spend in the presence of Antoinette, I deeply realize how unique and precious her spirit is in my life. I know someday, she will not be just a phone call away, she will be accessible in the realm of a subtler form. I still myself and send her and the connecting spirit my gratitude within. She is quite literally a light for me. She has never suggested she is my master teacher or queen, she so graciously conveys loving guidance and friendship, an offering of authenticity. I will honor her always, in whatever dimension I may find myself. After seeing her recently, I began to search and study the things my intuition spoke to me as valuable. It should be apparent by now that I don't limit the subjects or approaches to which I glean gainful knowledge. I know many organized religious traditions frown upon saturating one's thinking with multiple approaches, I must disagree. As long as one can develop objective discernment, he should be keen enough to peer into whatever his psyche is ready for.

Upon, a slow and peaceful waking state, I began to see aspects of light I had not seen before. I know almost all cultures, near and far, have or do worship light. Most revere the golden power source, the sun. In whatever name or person people put upon it, it seems to cut and design their mind. This is simple acknowledgement of the most obvious natural power to man on earth, but is this a negative practice? Verily, I say no. Worshiping light is not inherently bad, but it should be understood that light has the power to both reveal and conceal. Remember the sun can be blinding and burning, with overexposure. Be present. Also, the term light has dual meaning, as the lighter densities have brighter signatures of glow. We should recognize the brilliance of the night sky with all the glistening of star light, only available to our mind's eye in the cool darkness. The contrast of light is the spectrum and somewhere in that spectrum will always hide what we humans cannot see (with the eye), the dark. But be not afraid, for we dream in the night and we must be without fear of our dreaming subconscious state, it is but the necessity for or balancing conscious state. The tonal and the nagual are the coin of existence and will always reside in union.

Antoinette is an authentic human to me and I am thankful to have an example of one, otherwise I may never know how to recognize such vibrations. To live an inauthentic life is the avoidance of our deeper emotion, our true feeling. In our lives we do this to avoid pain but in so doing, we also negate our ability to feel pleasure. This is self-mutilation, cutting yourself off from your own nature of being. We have to willingly feel our darkest emotions in order to become our true authentic self. Authenticity is balance; time with eternity, soul with ego, and creator with creation.

The will is the key strength in building the soul temple, its foundation is always love. Man has such deep self-awareness that he has developed his will, so much he sees his freedom of will. This divine power must be cared for responsibly, must be aligned with the tune of the nature around him. Man, often with science wrongfully thinks he can dominate himself and the natural world but with true deep study we learn that nature and the system of cosmic order needs not us to bountifully proliferate. She knows exactly when, how and where to design beauty and eternal harmony. Man will eventually see his body temple is designed with his free will and intent to evolve embodied consciousness in the same fashion. We will only suffer when we attempt to dominate or rigidly control our temple or the nature within us. As stated before, man is the originally technology to willfully be the cosmic harmonic. Daily action in stillness, meditation, prayer, or recapitulation is how we rid ourselves of the chatter of the past, thus balancing our four bodies and cleaning the temple. Cleaning, sanitizing is sanity. The most sane and cleanest place to reside is the present moment. As William Blake poetically put it; "When the doors of perception are cleansed, man see things as they are; infinite".

What western man calls Solomon's temple is really the soul of man's house (his human form), and must be taken care of with authenticity and truth, in order to bring it to Earth, the ground of being. There are 4 aspects of light symbolizing the natal figure. This is why the number four is sacred it is light's design of expression in direction. Example, four winds, four directions, four corners, four triplicities, four elements. In light, division exists to make polarity and correspondence as law. Division is rest and radiance at the same time. This division opposes itself in light as north/south axis and east/west axis, creating balance, dimensionality, duality, and equilibrium. This in man is also the creation of the deific mind, divine ego. It is not something to be destroyed; it is something to be consciously and keenly balanced. When divine ego, is fully aware, it is not fearful or destructive. Centering your consciousness here is an apophatic process, meaning it is a negation of all that is false, and then revealing what is real or true. Figulus speaks it this way, "bodies cannot be changed except by reduction into their first matter". The gospel of Thomas says it his way; Jesus, Iesus said, "When you see your likeness, you rejoice. But when you see your images which came into existence before you, which neither die nor are made manifest, how much will you bear?" From this light plasma, is born the densest enfoldment, material nature. In nature, all material forms are of the expression of crystallization, it is the light arc of sleep or death, but not non-existence for in dying is the birthing from the current womb into the next. All bodies dissolve into another or greater cosmic expression, and in the highest states of consciousness, crystallization occurs no more, and beauty remains.

You are infinitely more than you know yourself to be. When you agree and see this simple truth you must then ask yourself, is it possible to discover more of this active infinity within? Antoinette and I were discussing the syncretic reintegration of all of histories written knowledge when she made me keenly aware that my retainment and dispensation of factual information is very worthy and important but how does it matter to others? What do all the syncing and connected dots do for other people when they listen and engage with them? I realized it means we are infinitely more than we are currently taught or know ourselves to be and we decide when we are ready, to move out of our own way and move into our hearts to remember our center, or unimaginable potential. And when we do, by Jove, lightning strikes. She said, when people engage in the search for the true religion, or better yet, the search for truth they have to realize it is a unifying endeavor. It is essentially not possible for one to see truth if they are themselves split, fragmented, or not whole. Man's real quest is that which increases his ability to participate with spirit, move in tune with spirit, to see spirit within ourselves and feel it with others and to experience the vibration of love. Ultimately all spiritual traditions are seeking this, a conscious and deeper participatory awareness of spirit. If you want to measure whether or not you have made any progress in this quest, ascertain if you are more authentically yourself then you were before.

She went on. Can we begin to entertain that we are more than what roles we play, more than our titles, and more than our histories, even more than our cultural dress? Will we open our minds and hearts for just a moment to the possibility of our deepest potential? This is what all true paths offer us as sentient beings. But will we respond? Will we ask ourselves if we are willing impact our beliefs enough to contemplate ideas (I-dios) that will shift our awareness to interact with reality in a new way, a way we were un aware of before now? Will we be ready to re-think our paradigms truthfully enough to expand them, enough to affect our being? I remember just outside the cave, Thot boldly asked me "who are you"? I spoke a name, a mask, a persona and all in truth but who am I, who are we, what purpose are we designed? To answer honestly, I absolutely must consider the infinite order in which is revealed and reflected here, now.

The goal, is to become awake, not to follow a previous person's path. To do so, you will hopefully understand the freedom needed is not given to you by any outside force or description. It is gifted to you when you diffuse the light of your paradigms, and unbind your consciousness. Are you willing to be with the idea of the direct perception of your being? Man's destiny is unity consciousness, and if we currently don't see it this way, I certainly think we will upon the moment we drop our physical body and integrate our being into dying. Without the body, binding and limiting our perception of being, unity must become so obvious. Man becomes aware of this by recognizing first that he is a spiritual being. Once there, it is so obtuse to think that he ever forgot this at all. We have our own seed of divine regenesis enfolded within. It's a spiritual motion, a *spiral-ritual*, remembering the sacred spirals of the awareness cycles.

The spiral-ritual or the ritual of spirals is the remembering of the road back home, the red road, the road to the still point or center of being. Awake, or remember you've been asleep, Walk beyond the cave. In the light that fills the room, shines out from Antoinette, it cascades directly out of her body, and showers in my direction, I found myself in stillness, and consciously realized I am awake. I felt a stirring within me, an answer to the dream I have been floating in.

She spoke of golden light filling the room as she asked me what I was seeing. Like most times before, I witnessed huge amounts of radiant light and luminous beings coming through her. I asked if she knew who they were and she said, spiritual masters and other people too, possibly relatives, all in blessing. Foolishly, I asked if they were good spirits. She smilingly replied yes and went on to say that if you see the spirits in the light, this glorious radiant light, they are most certainly powerfully ascended and benevolent and that the light works in this way. No negative forces can come through or have access to the light. I know she is right. The light flowing through her is a natural beauty that I remember from the original maneuver of creation and that light remembers me. There is only benevolence in this eternal relationship.

9

Character of Reality

walked in the door to my tiny yellow kingdom. I was content, just rolling around the thoughts of the day, as usual. My habit had me gulp down a cool mouth of fruit juice and drop my bag to start a moment of decompression. For some reason, I easily fell into a trance, a space between breaths. I met Thot in my mind, but I was not dreaming, I knew exactly where I was. I was sitting on my bed, upright and my vision was inward.

The evening had just begun, so it was dim in my dwelling. A picture begins to form in my mind. It's dusk and I am overlooking a meadow while sitting on a large granite rock, like the ones from the pastureland of my childhood. The rock must be the size of a small house and needed to be scaled to perch upon it. Thot is standing to my right on the ground. He is cloaked in a dark robe, and has his walking staff which is different than before. It is bent like a shepherd's hook but with feathers and fur covering the curved part. Also a web encircles the hook with a small solar cross made of bone suspended in the middle.

He tells me to tune in, and that he will help me in this endeavor. Tune in to what, I asked? Focus your gaze on one of those small trees across the field and see each individual leaf as it moves in the wind. I said I can't even see one leaf from this distance and I looked down at the rock I am sitting on. He gives me detailed instructions on how to pull my attention across the field and be able to see the tree, with absolute clarity and from close enough to smell its scent. I listen intently while noticing boulders with lichen in many shades of pale green and grey making ruffles and patterns of new growing lichen and stains from older clumps that were once there. The rock is a splash of thousands of patterns in shades of similar grey. I relax and see the rock again as just one big dark bolder and this make me concentrate.

He tells me to do it, do it now, practice your gazing to see the rhythm in the nature in which you are luminously linked. I looked up, and across the meadow. The tree I picked, maybe an ash tree, is medium and pulled me into it. I feel my attention warp the space of my vision and the view wrapped around me beyond my peripheral vision. In this way the tree widens and appears to be wrapped around me. It reminds me of a magnifying glass only I am not holding it. The magnifier is the tree somehow looking at me. I get the sense that the tree is somehow holding me under a magnifier which brings me close enough to see every leaf and the details of the striation of the bark upon the tree trunk. I felt a hum in my body and knew my perception of reality was shifting. I have felt this humming vibration before, sometimes subtly on my own but certainly when in the presence of Antoinette.

Thot spoke to me and said what do you see? I immediately snapped back into my normal attention, back across the meadow. My body wriggled with a chill, and I gasped my breath. He chuckled and said oops, with the sound of a grin, though I couldn't see his face in the darkness. Knowing I was questioning what had happened he offered a description of what occurred within me. He said, "the eye be single and full of light. I am sure you've heard this phrase, this is what happens when the eye is single, you can see!

Your eyeballs are two, so they perceive the world around you in dual, the description they create is dualistic. But the eye in reference to the old phrase is the eye of the mind and it uses the tool of intent in order to see and create. This single eye is much older and the parent of the two eyes on your face. The single eye sees the world around you and within you in union, this is why you vibrate. You are feeling the connection you have with all of the reality you perceive. This eye defragments the world and unifies it, renders it as it is, in wholeness. Your body is split in two, and so your dualist design is how most people see the world but when the eye is single a deeper and intrinsic view of truth is revealed. The main purpose for this view is to remind people that consciousness is never divided. The psychologists use fluffy languages to divide consciousness into id, ego, and subconscious but these are mere descriptions. As they learn to see, it becomes clear that consciousness, albeit ever in motion and flux, is unfolding that leaves no divisions. A wrinkle, is just a rolling wave, not a division. He went further into this and said what happened to you just now took much more time and energy than you know, you must remember how to do it from now on. Your reality will never be as it was before. You must remember how to harness the energy of aligning consciousness with reality as it is.

When this happens your eye is single and full of light, the light is the connecting force; it connects the observer to the observed. He is open, he has found and focused the dial and tuned it to the inner voice beyond, the sound intrinsic. He has found the channel in the harmonic frequency to the original sender creator. His eye, ears, and other senses are so turned on they look through the volume, the cube of time. The eye is so open it pulls all sight in. He moves through reality seeing it as all mind, living mind. An expanse so grand, the end does not exist. In order for him to tune the channel, he navigates using the senses but only for information, this is an intellectual pursuit. The rest is psychic and intuitional. He then uses the little cone in the brain, vibrating behind the eyes. It vibrates to the note of the universal expanse, the one verse. He remembers this note, and its experience and knows he has felt it and seen it before. It was so intensive that his world shifted from the tuning. Such a shift is so powerful he cannot express it so it becomes stored in the emotion and dream of his body. The lovely sound of lightning bolts in the brain causes his remembrance.

The channel of the expanse not only comes into his being; it connects to his being causing him to vibrate at the tuned expanse. The connection energizes his being and moves through him so that he may experience even more. He becomes able to reflect his expanse by seeing it with his senses and express it with his heart as a gift back to the expanse. As gratitude for life the expanse sustains him as he reflects in grace. When he has stopped reflecting he has either lost focus or lost his ability to harvest energy. Both are detrimental. When his reflection becomes foggy he must retune but also must beware that the channel is now slightly different because it now includes the nuances of his previously gifted reflections. In this way the channel is ever changing and ever new. He poignantly withdrawals from his senses and focuses on the vibration of the universe. The universe is reflected in the skin of a water drop gently gliding down the length of a leaf, it changes as it moves yet always reflects the entire cosmos. What's inside and outside the drop are the same. The body layer that holds the drop unto itself is temporary, illusory and unique to the material plane. When the drop evaporates or smashes inside out of the form of grace, it loses its conscious focus on the channel, until it remembers deep within its essence the intrinsic union with the eternal expanse. It's a mystical dance between humility, intimacy, and love.

The cone in the brain can become overwhelmed by mind, but this is an evolutionary nudge because the cone constructs the dream within man and universal mind is never in decay. Man's cone does decay as it is in the physical body. Even still, the cone constructs the dream and can shift, design, and create at will but it needs to draw on the energy of the heart. Because the will is only present in the heart. The heart pumps and powers the motivation to live and the desire to construct the dream. It is a kin to the sun of the solar system, it is radiant, and bestows love to all that is. Without the heart, we never wake up, we only sleep."

His words stuck to me as I knew I needed to heed the message, I intuitively knew what he was telling me was going to help me. I felt myself impulsively needing to remember to remember. I told myself to write it all down when I could reach a pen and paper. I fell deeper in the thought of what core ideas have been gathered and enfolded in my memory of being with him. I spoke to myself and calmly made it clear that no matter how long it was before I got the opportunity to document these core concepts, I would somehow remember them. I spoke them to myself; *the core voice is silent and can always be accessed in the present moment. **As above, so below, every form in the universe is transforming itself through mediumship from still point, to tiny, and to infinite; we are the micro version of the infinite macro. All consciousness is interconnected and therefore unified, even if it doesn't appear so. The nature of consciousness is specular, thus reflects back to us the face we shine into it. The body is the temple of God. To realize knowledge or know thyself is an apophatic process; the self is something one creates not something one finds.*** I somehow knew these perceptions were now a part of me. I embodied them and would clearly be able to recall them when necessary.

Thot laid out before me such deep psycho-spiritual knowledge I felt grateful, he decided to go on with the mind. He said, "the ancient Toltecs stood in the light of the sun and truth and systematically looked at themselves as reality revealed itself to them. This is what Planet Earth must do now in this time, as the water bearer is becoming the sign behind the sun and brings honesty. This is their greatest gift to themselves and mankind. Not to say that they were perfect and without their massive mistakes, but they faced the fear and shadow that lies within every human luminous being until progress and greatest flood upon man, the flood of consciousness. The natural process of higher mind awareness will be quickened in this time and the marker of the little planet Pluto aides with the psychic cleansing in its 250-year cycle.

As the Toltecs looked inside their mind in union with solar consciousness and universal mind thinking, they became aware of their death. In this is great power they began to commune with the spirit of their death and came to know it intimately. They developed an eminence when they claimed their awareness of personal power. Communing with death shined lights of brilliance on the nature of the psyche and the fragmentation within. Seeing the death of the body is an opening for the mind to move into deeper reality, it is how they discovered that energy is immortal. Energy cannot die, it only transforms and so they know they are made of energy and the awareness within it. All the forms that energy goes through only show the connection to everything. Through this, they came to know that the mist on the lake and the dew on the morning stones, through universal mind, are precipitates of awareness.

In the connection to everything, in mind they transcend psychic neurosis, they defragment and so integrated into reality now, the present moment. They also learned to not need or seek the approval of others and in this a massive step forward because when you no longer seek the approval of others you no longer subjugate yourself to their control. They became a small culture of individuals to be sovereign of mind, which disintegrates all politics and the illusion of inequality of peoples. Sovereignty of mind loves and respects others as equals. And one cannot come to selfhood by being dependant on others or their approval of you.

That evening I slept, and was found lucid again in the dream. The nagual, that infinite part of me began to show a darkness within me, so terrifying. It appeared as a dark spirit with smiling violence. It had no form or gender, just movement and wrath. I was in a room and back to the wall. I realized I am lucid as soon as I surveyed the environment. It's just an empty room, hardwood floors and dim but not too dark. Hanging from the ceiling is a light blue satin ribbon. The ribbon has a large triangular shaped weight holding just above the floor. It's wooden looking and rounded, it has a sheath encasing it that looks like husk from corn. Immediately it is imbibed with an evil spirit and tilts itself slightly at an angle, maybe sixty degrees. This is not normal behavior for gravity bound objects, so I know it is maleficent. Boom, it flies at me faster than I imagine, many times. Back and forth towards my head, maybe nine or ten times, relentlessly. There is no face but an overwhelming feeling of sinister violence. I jolt back into my bedroom, where I am in the room but out of my body. I am in between the physical realm and the astral, I hover and feel ripples of waves move through my body. The waves are painful but somehow reveal themselves necessary, as if resolution will occur through them.

Thot comes to me, and says "Just as you are made in the divine mind of God, this violence is made of your divine mind. You have an opportunity."

I was of anxious fright but knew exactly what his message meant. I had felt my body wriggle with these pain sensations for years and I knew I could change things. Breathing heavily, my energy pulsed above my bed and I called upon the great masters I have seen with Antoinette. I surrounded myself with white light in the form living flame and I held this image in my mind's eye as I called them and the great spirit and grandmother earth. This battle went on. The ribbon spirit laughed and divided my thoughts and said I had no protections and that I was a lie to myself, and brought up very dark images of terror, death, war, and perverted symbols. I heard my own voice say, turn it around, turn it around. I proclaimed that I am light, still casual light and I am the only one who holds the power to change. I knew then, that this destructive force was a foreign installation from a younger time of my mind and I didn't know what its name was but that I have dominion over it. I proclaimed to it that it is not welcome here and never will it attempt to return for it knows I have banished it with light. It stood before me in furious anger and fumed, as I spoke to it. I said you now know that your power is only illusion and of deceitful lies, you are the divider of mind but I am whole. I am unity consciousness and you have no power here and never will. I turned up the light in the room and flooded it.

Still in a heightened state of awareness and intensely shaken, I went over to the ceiling to untie it's fixture, knowing if it lashed out again it would not be limited or tied down. My heart pounding, I moved toward the fixture and woke up heavily in my body, in my bed. It took some time for me to come to a normal bio rhythm and normal breathing pattern. I stood up, cleansed my body with sage and honored the four directions, the great spirit, and those beautiful luminous beings that came to aid once again, showing their love and interest in my sanctity. I knew this dark spirit was hiding in the recesses of my personal mask, my personal mind and now has been forced into the scrutiny of the holy light. It shrieked in cowardice as its true nature was revealed to my higher mind. I saw the abused and confused fear as small and only serving me as such, a curled up baby boy in pain. Being the power of the nagual, the dream world and in the waking world as well. I affirmed to myself that I would never be as I was in the past. I am now center, standing in the medicine wheel, seeing simultaneously in all directions. I will never feel the original pain again, that pain is gone. I may feel another pain, but not that one. I will never be powerless, the waves have settled into the stillness of light.

I was waning, in between states of awake and sleep. The light had washed me. Thoughts came flooding to my mind as a bundle of information. The human eye is the vesica Pisces shape, it is an almond, it is the shape of womb, and light entering the eye is a sexual act. The light hitting the retina as it penetrates the eye is as the phallus entering the womb. In nature it is the process of regeneration of reality. As the light exposes reality to the nerves of the brain, that which is observed becomes the observer. Metaphysically be mindful of that which you gaze upon for you will become it. Realize that all you take in with the eyes are of a dual nature and only become conscious when the mind/thought acts upon them. Much of what we see goes to the unconscious because we can only focus on a certain amount at any given time. We must become aware of what is seeping into the unconscious in order to resolve this chaos.

Nothing can be brought to an end or resolution in the unconscious. Things must become conscious in order to be dealt with in the present moment. Our conscious mind is always being met by our unconscious in order to get us to integrate into reality. So if you carry pain in your body you must become conscious of it to end it, your body is speaking to you. You must be willing to engage in the dark night of the alchemy of the soul. It's our resistance to the cycles of the dark winter that amplifies their own suffering. If you go into winter with acceptance you suffer but you suffer with poise and grace, you live in wholeness and truth. When an inner situation is not made conscious it comes to us and appears outside as fate. Meaning all repression and avoidance of our true self, our whole self, causes our darkness to conspire to meet us in order to force us to integrate into wholeness as a conscious person.

Of all doors you walk through in the mind, you must bring your consciousness and integrity with you. The door will close upon it if you choose to leave it outside. The door will close and sever it in pain. The pain and suffering screams at you to take off your mask, your persona, and be limitless. Man collectively is still to wake up in this world, the workings of his own wars against himself and see he alone can stop his psychic destruction by willingly turning up the lights within the room of his heart. You must learn how to give to yourself, give love, wisdom and divinity, know thyself. The heart is paramount in this process.

Dedicate your life towards truth and dedicate the mind to the heart, all virtue and creativity lies in the heart. The mind is a useful servant of the heart and not the other way around. Knowing comes from the heart, while thinking comes from the mind. When the heart is injured, it is injured by thought or emotion, psychic damage also occurs. The Sovereignty of body, mind, and spirit exist only in the peace of the heart. Defragmentation of the mind/psyche occurs only in the heart. What is your dream, where is your dream for this life? You'll find this not in your mind, but the answer lies in your heart. The rhythm song of a heart is the barometer of life force and spiritual progress in man. Egyptians ceremoniously weighed the heart in judgement. If your heart was light, you were permitted to pass to the heavens. When weighed on the scales upon death, it is to be as light as a feather.

Not knowing how long I've been lying down in these deep contemplations, the words of Hermes funneled into me. I had been recently studying Principles of the Hermetica "He who understands that nothing rests and everything is in vibration grasps the scepter of power.... Spirit is the infinite living mind. Nothing can rise higher than its source. So man in the image of God is God only by degree. Man is finite living mind". Only when man becomes a higher degree does he become infinite living mind or spirit. Causal still light is different. It causes movement but does not move as it is the cause; the stillness and infinite light does not travel, does not move. It is still, it is causal. The movement of light as a wave is just photon particles reproducing themselves in the shape of spirals, in toroidal fields; giving rise to the illusion of movement.

I realize then, that I remember studying the Toltec teachings, and their idea of truth and lies. As they say, heaven is when our spiritual eyes are open. The Garden of Eden was heaven on earth until we ate from the tree of knowledge, this is a metaphor. God asked us not to eat from the tree and there were two trees, the tree of life and the tree of knowledge. The tree of Knowledge is also known as the tree of death. The story of light or fallen angels also is known as the princes of lies whom told us to eat. Everything he (the deceiver, the one who only seeks power over others) says is a lie, including his statement telling us to eat. We ate so from then our source of knowledge is all lies. Fragments! Whoever eats the fruit will have knowledge of good and evil so we began to judge right and wrong. It was a lie, so we believe it, so we separated from our true nature, God. We now need to ask ourselves who is the one in your head that judges? Who has all the opinions? The voices in our head never stop and it is mostly lies. This is why we don't see heaven, our spiritual eyes are closed. The big liar takes over the dream of our lives. We create a dream of humanity, individually but our will first creates individuality. It is the original fragment before fragmentation as a whole. We were our authentic self, our whole self, before we believed in the original lie which is what fragmented the unconditioned consciousness.

We must stop the internal dialogue to stop the duality, and defragment. We uphold our reality with our internal dialogue. We actually create and manifest reality but each moment is new, so our internal dialogue always exists in the past, in our memory. In order to create truth and reality, we have to stop our internal dialogue, and tap into the present moment which is truth. We believe the conflict of the universe is about good and evil, it is not. It is the conflict about truth and lies. The original lie (which is very deceptive) gives rise to the lie of good and evil. Believing in lies creates injustice and hate primarily within oneself then reflected on others. Truth creates love and happiness. If you agree to believe in something your faith is now invested, faith is very powerful. Truth can only be experienced, it cannot be put into words, this is why the name of God is unsearchable or unfathomable or unnameable. It encompasses all. If we put truth in words, the truth becomes a description of truth and is distorted. However, we have to communicate somehow.

Our heads are full of stories, our description of the word. We can't judge others because they are always believing in their own story. Everyone's story is just the description of the world, their truth. The program of knowledge is handed down to us as children. Before we have words and programs in our hands, we are pure spirit, we are our authentic self. As children our society constantly tells us who and what we are or should be, this is fragmentation. The main lie we believe is that of our own imperfection. We are told that we are born in sin, but this is a part of the lie. This affirms only that we are not great, not perfect and in a state of lack. So this lie is reinforced by our culture. Work, work, be productive and strive. We spend our entire lives in the state of lack. We're forgetting our perfection our wholeness our own connection to spirit.

You are dreaming the world you live in. You create the world you live in by holding your reality in your internal dialogue. We are all here to create awareness when we create our dream. We are pure awareness the rest is illusion. The world of effects is differentiated light, not causal still light. When we witness the truth, the lies in our head cannot survive. This is frightening, but this is knowing. This fear is the first enemy of a man of knowledge. Fear gives way to clarity. You are the dreamer of your story, so the main character is real and true but what you believe about yourself may not be true. It may be just a hologram you agree with others to tell you about yourself. But it is an agreement.

We can only know the story that we create about ourselves. Focus your attention on your own story, change what you believe about yourself; change yourself and everything in your dream changes. Dreaming the story of your life is the art of living. You're the author, but if you're inner voice is always talking, then who is listening? This is why you can't believe the voice, it is everything that makes

up the tree of knowledge so it is the prince of lies, the first
fragment. The integrity of your spirit is the truth, and the
truth has no voice, it has no language, it just is. Every time
you judge yourself, criticize, or guilt yourself, you're listening
to the voice of lies and you believe it. This is your own
emotional abuse. Your own fragmentation. We are only a
step away from wholeness, which is knowledge without
thought. Stopping the internal dialogue is attunement. Stop
the liar. Stop believing the voice. Don't believe others, they
lie to themselves so they lie to you. You must keep an open
heart, in order to have an open mind. This will purify your
belief system, which is everything in your personal tree of
knowledge. Listen to the story but don't believe it. Stop that
voice, if only for a moment and awareness will change, the
reality you create will change.

The DNA, which is light sensitive, absorbs light and
emits light in the spiral of the sine wave. The DNA is likely
a holographic projection. All atoms have an extremely brief
transitory existence being holograms. We are life force, the
force that creates everything and every moment. The force
that moves our body, we are that force. Think of the reality
that is made of the reflection of emotions, for example. This
entire reality is the feeling of exchanging energy with
everything; all the birds, people and flowers, it's a reality of
feeling. With our spiritual eyes open, we see the story of our
internal dialogue fall away. We no longer connect with our
story. We erase our personal history even for a moment. We
connect with life force itself, we cannot describe the life
force because then it becomes our story again. Still we know
it is there, our spiritual eyes are open.

I am not sure if the Toltecs spoke of DNA, but this
reference to DNA applies to their philosophy. What they did

speak of was impeccability. This is a state of mind and being that leads man back to wholeness. Impeccability results from a balance between our inner world with the outer world/cosmos. "To be tempered and in tune with the will the Eagle's emanations. You must be persistent to be apathy. What is said to be magic is the long sustained intent beyond what seems possible, desirable, or probable. This loosens the rigidity of our limits, very few are willing to go this far. Doing this harvests and creates an abundance of energy. This leads to huge resources of power. The warrior must be in total control of his emotions because mixing power and clarity can be explosive. You cannot abuse power or it will destroy you. Intent is the tuning of our attention to the cosmic awareness which is what transforms our volition into commands of the Eagle's emanations. Once here, intent allows Seers to live in a non-ordinary world, a non-dualistic world, a world of wholeness, and this is where one can intend the destiny of total freedom"-Armando Torres

The voice of the heart calls to the heavens. Permit me not to perch or perish with the king who has ruled life for a day, this is the mind. But preserve me eternally in my ruler ship of the infinite. This is the heart. The mind may become infinitely more genius but without heart you will become infinitely more subversive and fragmented. It is the heart that unifies consciousness and is solely responsible for the creative process. And mind is only noble when employed by the heart. All schisms and schemes dissolve within the truth in light, transcend the insecurity of the ego and bring man consciously to himself. The vibrational signature of such a person is fearlessness, some may call it love. When you meet one of these people they are awake. Man is a star bound to a body and the inner light burns as a fire within. Number and numerical literacy gives birth to the logos, the Word of God. For numbers are the original linguistic symbol in matter, all graphics are built upon them. Order and balance are the law of the cosmos, Follow the law and you shall be one with all. Be aware of whichever form of slavery you choose to agree with. What limitations or cages that you agree to, these you build up around your mind. What catastrophe did you elicit in order to avoid your true nature? What illusions of separation have you bought into? See these illusions, then pause with them in between breaths, see you there in true power and let go of them, move beyond them, Into the depths of knowledge, your authentic self"(Manly P. Hall). I rolled over, knowing my own clarity, although frightening, it gave way to a small dose of power. In my sleep I asked myself, am I still sleeping? Should I wake up?

I inhaled deeply and sunk into my bedding. Lights flickered. All motion arises from stillness and so is but a simulation or symptom of universal stillness. We divided motion and so see more symptoms but when we divide stillness we create motion. The source of all motion is stillness and so light is the same, it is born of stillness. Still magnetic light is causal and we only detect it once in motion. Once in motion it is transformed into electric light. All manifestation is electric light. We transcend our manifested vibration by attaining stillness. Here we enter the cause, we are cause. He is the domain of divine will. Will is transcendent nature and accessible to us all. It is not of heart or mind, it is a universal center of all still points. It emanates from the core of our being and this is why the will is so incredibly powerful. It offers us the power to shape our own personal cosmology. It transcends polarity and as such is the grand equilibrium of being.

I rolled over again and realized I was waking. My body was completely at rest and in peace. The notion dawned on me, in my dream of the dark ribbon, I survived by commanding my own sovereignty, I offered myself my own light. The light of wholeness, the spirit. The next thing that entered my consciousness was the morning sun.

10

Light of Egypt and the Body

On the floor, sitting in my way to decompress my lumbar spine against my bed I sit with a belt around my knees as they are pulled in toward my chest, like a sitting fetal position. The belt lets me relax and not have to hold my knee in with the lower pelvic muscles, over time the spine decompresses. I start my mornings this way next to a brilliant hot coffee with a touch of cinnamon. Sitting in silence, I remembered I just dreamt. Thot came to me in that dark cave, he appeared and said come out of this hovel and I will educate you on the holy temple and show you the temple of light. I obliged, just a mental thought to get up and step toward the cave entrance, and I was there. The entrance always has a specific smell, I can never discern exactly what it is, a blend of creosote and hickory or something similar.

We sat at the entrance just outside the overhang of the cave; the slap of drops of water slinked and slapped the ground behind us, in small puddles. The air was crisp and moist, it was pleasant. He sat with his pipe and began to teach. He said, "calm yourself and listen to the intent of what I share with you. Very few westerners ever come to realize the most primal and essential truth concerning their own cage. All life at its ground level is energy in motion and is imbibed with awareness, all is awareness. If you catch this truth in a state of self-realization, you will never forget it; the doors to the higher realms will forever remain open. Standing in the light of the sun, the ancient Toltecs know this most sacred knowledge. You already know the universal harmonizing principle of as above, so below. When we look up, we see the cosmos, it is the macrocosm, and you Ram, the fish, the dragon, Little-King-Bear, the smoke by the creek, are the microcosm. You are it, the all of it. When you see this simple fact, you are in universal mind consciousness, satori, crystalline or Christ consciousness. When this happens, the original differentiated split of still casual light comes back together as wholeness. This state of being is love.

Look up and see with your two eyes the sun, and see with thy single eye the unification of that sun within you, for it is the power of all the cosmos and as its rays stretch down to you, you are that light itself in a human frequency. The sun is the creator of all energies, bodies, and planets in our solar system. It births the planets from its equator just as human do. They start as subtle rings then spin intensely into planets. Here, the earth is expanding and your day has been, for almost 3,000, years measured at 365 days. The numbered order of things up there is reflected down here. The temple of God is the human body and the kingdom of heaven (up there) is the higher mind of universal Kryst consciousness. All great sages and masters of light, the true yogi and sundancers know this and hold this as sacred. Earth is symbolized as rest, fire as motion, the fire within the heart of man is the only bridge to higher mind. The motion gives rise to time as a relative factor.

Unifying heart with time, this is occurring when the crown chakra is polarized in harmonic union with the heart. This is eart**H**/**H**eart uniting with spirit/eternal time. Lovingly, shed your selfish/fearful and align your personal will with divine will, Align your luminosity with the divine vantage of the eagle's emanations.

Those essences we create and cultivate within our own soul, we can attract to us from the heavens. As the sun is the light in our heart the moon is in our bodily tides. The light of the celestial cosmos triggers the chemical wedding of our human bodies and runs the alchemical changes of the seasons of consciousness. In numerical and divine order, the tuning of man to the science of light has been power since the original man. All the religions on Earth and their heroes are all the stories of the light of the stars from age to age, ego to ego, and culture to culture. When you tune your will to the light within, it becomes apparent that all spiritual stories are the tracking and numbering of the stars in the sky. There was a time, the golden age when most men were in a state of knowing, humanity was in a state of direct knowing. This was when the science of light synced all sciences into one and all scholars went to universities to learn all subjects of the universe. There was no fragmentation in the psyche of man; they were of universal mind thinking. Peoples all over the world knew the body is the temple of God.

This knowledge of the body housing the temple of universal light, God force and the power to co-create certain fibers of reality was mapped by the constellations of the zodiac. Even though people have all but forgotten this, it is still in order if you learn to tell the mazzaroth. Look up and see your own mind reflected in the spheres above. The ancient god Herne bestowed this wisdom on the druids and the Ari which became known as the aryans, meaning people of the north or people of the higher mind. They shared this knowledge of the movements and qualities of the planets with many kings and queens and this knowledge became the mystery schools. The shame of certain kings/pharaohs became corrupted by their own fear of loss of rulership, so they became split in the psyche and were easily persuaded and purchased by the dark and conniving politicizing people. I will tell you more on this at another time, just understand that the result is still here in modern peoples collective psyche as a history that is riddled with lies. Modern man is still yet to be told at least half more of the true history.

The zodiac marks the procession of the equinox as they concern the viewpoint of Earth. Most ancient sites and megaliths mark this in the sky as a calendar or a clock to keep track of the ages. Peoples encoded its cycle in the buildings to forever remain in touch with this cycle because this cycle runs straight through the human body in waves of light. Just as the sun's elliptical produces a sine wave from the tropic of capricorn to the tropic of cancer, the sun produces the same sine wave through you from head toe. The differences in the wave is only micro, so the information within this light is still exactly the same. The age of pisces has just ended and Yeshua/Jesus ruled it as the symbol of the fish. There has always been a man personified as the sun for each 2,160 years (an age). Twelve of these ages is the complete zodiac as it moves through the entire cycle over its completion of 24,000 years. So many people have forgotten this cycle but it is just as important as the 24-hour day, which counted as the earth orbits the sun in 365 of these days. Even a child sees the daily cycle as it becomes aware of nightfall and day rise. But they're not so aware of this action taking 365 days to make a year until they are taught by elders on each birthday. The larger cycle is the duty of the wise elders of sacred knowledge to impart the 24,000 birthdays time cycle on the children.

Each age carries with it specific angles and frequencies of galactic and solar light to hit the people of earth. Light is the provider of consciousness and turning on the lights causes darkness to flee, this happens in the mind of man because as I've said, man is the temple of God. Listen to these words and never forget again, your divine design as the microcosm *micro cosmos*. In your year of 2012 your sun and system crossed into the northern hemisphere of the Milky Way galaxy and the frequency of light here is much different than in the southern hemisphere. The sun is also in a binary elliptical orbit with a star called by Egypt as Sirius. This binary relates to the light and its effects on the earth people too. By the year 2,400 the golden age will be known and seen by most people on earth. The consciousness of the mind of man will be so aware of the harmonic frequency that harming others will be very rare because all is interdependent, so harming other life is understood as harming oneself.

As for now, the Age of Aquarius is beginning and this is the only sign of which takes the form of a man, all others are animal or of a hybrid nature. The Aquarian is the one who floods with water. It brings a new light vibration, which corresponds to new bodies. Old bodies that cannot adapt and contain the *new wine* will decay. You have chosen to come in this life and body to upgrade to this Aquarian light, this is why you have had such pain and struggle physically in your life, you have made great strides and harmony is yours as you will soon see. The pain is not only physical, it is psychic as well. There is a harvesting of souls to occur also, it's just as the spring flowers open and release their love to the light, so humans who vibrate in harmony release their body to give their souls consciousness back to light. This process is how the great spirit renews itself eternally. It creates light in order to sustain light ever new in each moment.

Flowers even resemble the sun in their form, they petal out in curved radiance as a unique reflection of solar consciousness. Man is no different except he has a free will, or conscious knowledge of God, so he must choose to love himself in order to renew. So in the age of Pisces the Christ consciousness said in your bibliography "If those who lead you say it is in sky, then the birds will precede you. If they say that the kingdom is in the sea, then the fish will precede you, rather the kingdom is inside of you and outside of you. When you come to know yourself, you will become known. Then realize it is you that are the sons of the living father but if you will know yourselves then you will dwell in poverty and it is you who are that poverty". The zodiac is outside of you and inside of you. On to the words of Thomas in his gospels of Nag hammadi, he says "Let he who seeks continue seeking. When he finds he will become troubled, when he is troubled he will become astonished. When astonished he will rule over all". Thomas, the twain is the twin and he becomes astonished to know that yes the kingdom is and always is within.

I was deeply mesmerized and I was about to bring up a question when Thot said, "are you aware that you are seeing? Be still, there in this moment you are seeing. He put his hand on my shoulder and said I hear your question, you've answered it by seeing. All knowledge comes in the stillness between time, you are there now, remain for a moment and listen. Your moment can last for as long as you intend it so. On to Egypt," he said. "Now Egypt is not the beginning but it serves as a wonderful model as a culture of higher knowledge. They were in a trade of higher knowledge with not only the east but the west and great knowledge was given to them by the shaman/priests of the land of Ireland from the druids. Look no further than early king Menes fulfillment of his burial in sacred Ireland. This is a thousand years before rise of eighteenth dynasty rulers. His daughter bears the name Scota for which Scotland is now named. I say to you when a message from heaven is heard it is first heard in Heliopolis (the heart), repeated at Memphis (the throat), Thermopolis (the head), then at Thebes (the crown). These are the cities on Earth that are established forever and remain in time and are the correspondence to the chakras from heart to crown or higher mind. The Egyptians built their sacred temples as huge monuments of the human form, so as to never forget the sun's light enlivens the earth just as it does the human body. The temples are designed as the body and even greater the Nile river itself serves from the sky as the brain and spinal column of the human being.

The land of Egypt or Kem is the chemical transformation known as alchemy which is not turning metal into gold but turning the human vices into virtues. Alchemy is the ascension process to higher consciousness, every human's birthright. Much of this knowledge will fly by your thoughts but when meditated upon, will reveal a natural mystic truth to all who have eyes to see. Look now at the symbols of the west world, we will stay with Egypt. The tetrahedron triangle is the heart center in the body and associates as fire, the transformative element. Two tetrahedrons encircled are the hermetic, hern, mercurial symbol when inverted so as to one facing up in masculinity and the other down in femininity. This symbol used by many cultures stems from the land of Kemet to unfold the union of male/female light into one original light of causal potential or stillness. It spins into genders creating new life through union or procreation. When conceived, the newborn is represented as a circle, complete and whole, no corruption. The still point or nucleus within is termed Isis, the radius extending out is termed Ra (ra-dius means light god), and the circle's edge is the god termed El (Elohim). These make up the 3 gods or aspects of the god holy trinity in the geometric and mathematical language of light and shape. The entire universe when drawn is only done so as a circle. The equations and vectors within the shape are a play of light and shadow known as sacred geometry. Look to the great minds of Plato and Pythagoras to meditate on geometry to raise your mind out of the left, through the right and into union of higher consciousness. All the gods are 3 and then back to 1 in Atum.

Be known that of the appearance of the planet Pluto now in the heavens near the year 2,000 for its reflected light is a psychic cleanser for the human. It will be present for some 250 years and uproot the old paradigm of fear and lack lodged in the psyche. It will reveal the beginning of the flood of consciousness leading to higher consciousness on earth. In man's current fear state of thought he still feels threatened by nature so he fights against her but will never conquer for she is the sustainer, she powers man and man does power her for she is the wife of king Sun. She is self-healing, you have to come to realize this within, by getting out of your own way and allowing the harmonic deep inside to resonate within your ears and heart. She teaches you that you as man are self-healing too but this knowledge has been corralled by the bad shepherds. They sought in the time of Akhenaten to corral the innocent sheep into forgetting that they are their own priests and priestess, they are their own shaman, built by design with the seed of regenesis within. These bad shepherds are of envy and their names are not important for they are always visible as the exclusive royalty. They are so envious of consciousness that they present themselves as kings and queens but embody no kingdom, their fruits are rotten with decay easily bought and sold with the transitory currency of money, They're schema is faulty as it does not have heart.

See, the cone pineal in the head is the chamber of light. It is synced to solar light and rhythm of life. The cone is the single eye, man learns to *see* with this eye all things in wholeness. When this eye is single, thy body is full of light. This optic chamber or thalamus resonates through piezoluminescence cells like a retina and reflect light around the chamber and back to the eye, like a crystal. This is known as Christ, krst, or krishna consciousness. When this crystallization is active the entire human body (the temple) crystallizes and vibrates with light. The cone is also the constructor and controller of the dream world and shifts the dream through light chemistry (alchemy) at will. This is the will or intent of the divine, the built in design of the divine. The key is that the will is only present in the heart. The heart pumps and powers the impetus to live and to continue to construct the dream. Without the heart we continually sleep, never awaken.

Just as in our body's physical state we are prompted out of sleepiness by the shining light. God is light, all is light, we are rays of the light. The all is casual light diving into magnetic and electric light in wave form. The wave of light gives rise to effects of differentiation called atomics particles. But the particles are matter and matter is illusion so only real in the realm of illusory effects. Still light is cause; light in motion is effect. Still light is knowing, light in motion is thinking. Light manifests the movement of effects into matter in cycle. The cycle in waveform becomes denser and denser until reflected in the corpus of man, then back through the cycle in reverse, back to casual light. The dissemination is as such; cause, pre-angelic realm, angelic, spirit, mental, astral, etheric, mineral, vegetable, animal, human, then returns. The human temple is the barometer of spiritual consciousness that is in the material realm. It is the only creature of this polarity. Man is both mortal body and simultaneously immortal spirit, thus the only measure of the middle path of creation. Conversely the body of angels are neither mortal nor material and so the state of consciousness reflects these states.

As the temple of light, nature builds the harmonic attunement of consciousness to higher consciousness through the form of number. This subject is very dense but the simple, need to know is this: All science and knowledge is enfolded within the sun's ecliptic, its path, movement, effects, and manifestation. Fundamental numbers of recurrence are 3, 4, 7, 12, and 40. Three is the trinity (Vishnu, Shiva, Shakti), triangle. Four is directionals, sine wave form (serpent), seasons, square. Seven the 7 key octave, visible planets, visible rainbow light spectrum, chakras, septenary, harmonic, and serpent through vibration, mind of man. Twelve mind of universe, one complete circle of Pi (360 degrees). Forty we will get to later, 7 and 12 encode the 12 constellations of the zodiac and the sepentary within. These birth all religions and myths, they are the sun's hero journey through the elliptical undulations of the galaxy.

The wave of the zodiac microcosmically runs through the human body and attuning to the natural movements of such naturally, raises the crystalline consciousness to house light. The head is the place heaved up, this is heaven or higher mind, mount zion, Hi ram, aries, Abram, brahma, cere brum, the ram, Amun Ra. The beginning of the nervous system, the river Jordan, the Ganges, the Nile. Our own higher mind manifesting its own regenesis is evolving according to our own state of consciousness. So back to number 12 in myth and religious tradition, this number is so common it is not coincidence. There are 12 powers of divine mind, 12 bodily systems, 12 apostles, 12 posts of the zodiac, 12 days of Christmas, 12 rowers on the boat of Horus, 12 builders, 12 mason, 12 sailors in the ship of Ra and so on, these are but a tiny few. They all represent the sun (son) in its elliptical through the heavens. All is light emitting differentiations into, culture, speech, language, art, and conflict. This is man's divine design to instruct his 12 disciples, disciplines, bodily systems toward the higher mind illumination. This occurs outside of the personality, as persona is a mask, this is why God is not to be worshiped in the human form or persona.

The divine mind descends into matter in this way, ever moving through the atomic structures of the platonic solids. Light changes its vibration accordingly to the plane of existence in which it's currently on. And so in science the atomic structure frozen water bears a geometric solid that coincides, and when water moves to liquid, then to gas, and so on its atom geometric solid shape changes accordingly. The human being does so the same, as he is the vibration of manifesting divine light in movement. The great Greek sophist states "Man is the measure of the universe". The soul descends in four differentiations, earth, air, fire, and water; these are the elementals of the sphere of life on earth.

Examining the movement is the human embryo, the cell and the first differentiation from spirit into matter. The nervous system is the first system to form, and the body slowly encases it. The nervous system is the antenna and sensitivity receiver of spiritual knowledge through consciousness. As the embryo becomes a body the feet touch the back of the head as the spinal column is liquid and supple. The solar light wave/sine wave imprints the being with a cadence or solar rhythm which becomes the bio-rhythm of the body's entire life. This light rhythm is due the rotation of the sun and its emission of radiations that set and harmonize the being with alchemical regulations of the health systems. If these rhythms fall out of harmony in life, the body will begin to decay in dissonance and disease.

Now there is much confusion and disconcertment in the psyche of western man about the word meaning called Christ. So, as I give you the knowing, be still and meditate upon thy wisdom. The temple is not made with saw or hammers though ancient writing, all convoluted and politicized, still say it so. Think it through, if thy temple is known to not be made with saw or hammer, then what of its structure and substance? As your ears have listened, it is the body of man that is the temple and she is made of Light in the flesh. The Christ is in western words the path to god salvation and in this thought it can only be within the temple, it resides within as all sacred knowledge does. The fearful split of the dualistic mind trained into self-slavery refuses to see the reality of light as oneness, as a whole. The human is not designed with some vicarious seed of growth lying outside himself, just as the sunflower seeds lie within, so does this natural law abide in man. John 2:11 19-22 "Jesus answered them, 'Destroy the temple and I will raise it up again in three days." He is referring to the temple of the self, the human body.

The Christ, krst, krishna, chrism, christus is the sacred secret within the cerebrospinal system. The christus oil begins in the head, heaved up, heaven, father ram. The cycle of oil pumped from head to sacrum and back to head cause conscious illumination and spiritual ascent. The pineal gland produces as positive fluid and the pituitary produces a negative fluid. Each corresponds to first masculine electric energy and then to negative feminine energy. One goes down the pingala and the other the ida nerves. The sacrum which is a fusion of 5 bones (the stone of scone) serves as a rocking pump to pressurize and pump the fluid back up toward the brain. The sphenoid bone in the skull acts at the upper pump to keep the rhythm ever circulating. They work in tandem with respiration teeter-tottering, pumping fluid around the brain and spine. This rhythm is the correspondence of solar pulse, respiration, heartbeat and electric nervous information all equalizing into harmony.

Each month when the moon is in the sun sign of the body, which is 2 and ½ days per lunar cycle (month) the reflected lunar light provides an electromagnetic pulse to the solar plexus of the body. The solar plexus is termed so as it is and always has been the seat of solar energy storage in the body, the plexus along the spinal cord harbors a small thimble or manger where the christus oil collects on its journey back to the brain. This moon, many say has no such power but yet know its secrets of regulation the ocean tides of the globe, and tides within the planting of seedlings, and the waters of the woman's menstrual and sacred sex cycle. The pulse/light of the moon is known so well and intimate by the body, yet the ignorant will ignore its pulse to the solar plexus of man. The short sighted error again not knowing that the heartbeat of a beating chest is average at 72 beats per minute and this is a solar regulation as well. It is the microcosm of the one-degree movement of processional stars moving backwards across the sky every 72 years. The psycho-physical lunar pulse electrically charges this oil to help it ascend like the mercury in a thermometer towards the brain. This oil is the seed of man also called the son of man, also called the logos and it is secret and thus the word secretion is derived from secret. This sacred secretion is born of pineal/pituitary, male/female, Mary/Joseph, Abraham/Sara, electric/magnetic in differentiation. Then mingles down the spine as a serpent and commingled to alchemically marry into a new chemistry of physiological power. Rising upward the kundalini energy ascends through the seven nerve ganglia centers or chakras to return to the brain. If the body is in well health the seed will be cared for enough to make the journey back to the lambdoid (lamb of god), back to the Sara-Abram (cere brum) and it's two hemispheres.

As the oil makes its way through the corpus colostrum it flows from the left side brain to the right side. If it is not charged enough with the electric pulse, it may not be a sufficient amount may not make it into the third ventricle which is where the prodigal son/sun rests in return. This third ventricle is the feeding point of the optic thalamus, where the pineal gland sits in fluid. If the oil resides within the left side brain, each human is vibrating only at the awareness level corresponding to the intellect and this critiques, labels, and compartmentalize reality for him, thus living without the powerful capacity of right brain intuition. Without the intuition science is left unconscious and fragmented and it's learned knowledge the same, thus serving only to create division or separation within the consciousness of the person.

As it crosses the vagus nerve and into the optic thalamus (where the pituitary and pineal bodies originally differentiated), it touches the optic nerve which is the lamp or single eye. It is also called the cave of brahma, where the christus is still or dead for three days until activation occurs and the chemical wedding commences. This process is the turning of water into wine and the cleaning of the blood, the new blood. This is the renewing of the twelve sacred cell salts (salvation) in the blood which keeps the body alkaline healthy and raises the vibratoy consciousness within, offering the potential shifts in awareness toward unity consciousness. The christus, Krst, christ, chrism, Krishna, Yes (sun) is the inherent seed of theological, biochemical, theological, psychic, astro-theological, physics of the light of the universe on the earth plane.

The optic thalamus chamber is the eye of Horus as a cross section of the human brain when split between the two hemispheres. There are two olive shaped organs at the base of the chamber towards the back of the brain stem; these are the pillars of Hercules (the sun hero). When fluid then passed through ushers in the flood of consciousness of the entire ebbing and flowing system. The human body, again, is the temple of light. And as Moses apparently raised the serpent above his head he means to tell us of the Vedic practices of the inward unfolding of life force within, raising the serpent life force up the chakra system to the high brain. When the clever adept adds up all the pedals in the drawn image of the chakra wheels, they add to 144 pedals of the first six. The seventh is called the one thousand petaled lotus. When multiplied 144 times, 1000 equates to the 144,000 who so fortunately see the *name of the Lamb of God* upon their heads (mount Zion). This is none other than the christus or oil illuminating the head of the optic thalamus.

He went on to say, this knowledge in olden times was known and not hidden, still it was difficult to claim as many were apathetic or lazy in their disciplines and desires for their own authenticity. Through times and cultures the mystery schools taught their purpose as a method of imparting the knowledge of immortality to an initiate. Through personal experience of communing with their own spirit of death, they intimately were given the knowledge that death is another illusion. It is a birthing into a yet larger dimensional womb; wrap your mind around this truth. The highest sages devised ways to bring initiates into this experience with their death. Then some sages died to be reborn, then carry this knowledge through to their new body or form. Seek the natural world around you to see that all bodies when atomic or celestial are dissoluble. All containers with boundaries are by design dissolved and disintegrated when their held-in consciousness exceeds them. The only body that is not dissoluble, is that of *nobody*, the boundless infinite…total awareness, omnipresent consciousness, total freedom.

But in religious doctrine, the scribes known as men, in their own ignorance of the divine nature of man, seek personal glorification, and through greed fashioned corruption of the truth. You know an instrument by that which flows through it. One only has to look at the sanctions of war, terror, and brutality to see the false wolves in sheep's clothing. They always sell themselves as the intermediaries between man and god. They have hidden the knowledge of the brilliant druids that all men and women are by nature, they're own priests. This is because they all have within them their own seed of regeneration of the slight spark within. These wolves have no right to the names in which they claim, they slowly and systematically degrade and grind the heart-fire of love into control and power. They are imposters selling a personal fetish for the real and natural christus, the divine fire within the hearts of man. Look back deep into the Abrahamic thought to see that his father Terach's vocation was that of a craftsman of idols, sold to kings, queens, and mother Circe for profit.

Knowing now we, descend through the harmonic chasm of seven spheres of planetary bodies which are the microcosmic chakras, we as light differentiate down to the earth/material sphere. Here we must learn to see with thy single eye in order to make the dualistic differentiations whole again. Seeing unity consciously within, shapes and co-creates our outward reality into the same unity. The platonic solids (geometries of shapes) given to us by Plato, are the elemental shape-states light vibrates through to ascend and descend from formlessness to form. These variations of light are the archetypes of organization and distribution of energy (light) by relationship. All forms, organic and inorganic from deity to the mineral are of mediumship. Meaning each receives and transmits knowledge from higher to lower, thus offering the chain of potential ascension from lower mentality to higher. They are mirrors to attract and reflect one's true light within into conscious awareness and ownership. Once ownership and full embodiment of knowledge occurs, it can be then potentially offered to another who is open and willing to receive. These are cycles within cycles, relationships within relationships."

Thot, spoke to me for what seemed like days, I had no real outlook of time, he said my assemblage point had shifted and that he pushed it into new places on my astral body to keep me in keen awareness of what he was teaching. He said that time, is the first to go, as it is only linear when preserved with the bodily senses, and is much more like folding water when not tempered by the body. He said, "one more thing about relationships; the body truly is the temple of god, encoded within it is the order of the universe. Man builds the piano which is number itself (pi= 3.14) a never ending circle. The instrument has evolved but in standard forms it embodies the harmonic scales relative to the human hearing. The 88 keys are divisible by the 28 phalanges of the human hand and is the eleventh number in the phi sequence. Meaning phi(1.618) is building nature in spirals. 88/28 equals 3.14, the pi. The beauty of the circle is a relationship of math, to geometry, to humans, to hands, to the human ear, to the human heart of moving music. Deeply encoded in the human body is always the house of god."

He said he will teach more on number later, then he went on to talk about the knowledge of the great sage, Hermes. "Rising to the higher mind we vibrate our voltage beyond that which the body can hold. Our soul ascends beyond the seven chakras into the eighth sphere; there we learn the potential for even higher. When bathed in the light of the higher mind the initiate is then called. When he heeds the call, he can move into the eighth sphere. To do so, he must sing the song of silence to attune himself to the vibration of stillness. In the stillness a chorus sings to him and offers a vision. Here he becomes a seer."

He began to recite Hermes, and I was deeply impressed as it flew through him as if by memory, as if he was experiencing the vision himself. "The mind of the great dragon, he sees, the dragon so powerful. The dragon does nothing to injure man, man is injurious to himself simply by being afraid of the dragon- the divine mind. He becomes upheld by the light. He sees the mists of matter devour the light, and sounds the word. The word is the mist. The light is still there but hidden within the matter. The word is the tower of universal law and expresses itself in seasons, structures, harmonies, elements, and cosmic seasons. Only seers can see the column of the law."

He paused, looked up at the moon, with two fingers gently pointing upward and his hand holding his heart, he said, "the summit of all knowing is truth; truth is total freedom." His eyes phosphorus with waving chemical glow, they reflected something, a depth I had never seen in someone. It was as if he was looking at something a trillion light years away. The most high is still casual light, without differentiation. Truth is muddied and obscured by the illusion of mortality. Truth is experiencing reality without the existence of the self and when personality ceases universality remains. Cognition of infinite consciousness. Man is constantly forgetful of himself, this is the game, the divine play or dream. He is the only creature that has to continually overcome himself to live in harmony. Like the buddhic mind, the druids valued memory over the written word. In their wisdom they knew that the great light of seeing stamps the soul with embodied knowledge. They knew that man is the temple of God. They were invaded by envious magicians and the cult of personality oppressed them through the written word. But the druids knew through seeing that the reincarnated soul in another vibratory state needs only to recognize/remember who they are to resurface the divine truth within.

He went on, and said that the druids were a highly evolved people who kept sacred knowledge of the temple of the human body in a school taught through mystery. They taught their wisdom to all who desired it with a true heart. The romans infiltrated the druid lands, corrupted the science, and installed their own god Saturnia and then Mithraism in place of the celestial sun. As time went on the romans conquered more lands, stole and controlled texts and writings by withholding education and literacy for the true seeker. And finally installing the current sun god Yeshua/Jesus. Borrowing from the Druids and the Egyptians, they became sun worshipers as well but refused to reveal the sun's story as it truly is in the celestial sky. Instead they concocted an edit convenient for the mass control of psychic thought and behavior. Never to reveal that long line of sun heroes that Jesus belongs to, marking the current processional age of the pisces in the zodiac.

Even the Hebrews lost their own remembrance of the Christ sun as their high priest was bought and corrupted just the same. In their Hebrew tongue Y (J)esus means sun god, *Yes* is the word for sun and *zeus* is the Greek god Zeus (in Latin dios) meaning god. Therein lies the numerical encoding of Jesus the sun; also through gematria when one knows the skills of this trade, encodes the diameter and radius of the sun king in the sky.

The historical list of the western sun gods is numerous and all their religious myths easily traced by knowing the hidden sacred knowledge of syncretism. Horus, ra, Dionysus, Mithra, Ahura Mazda, Enkei, Hern, Hermes, Enoch, Osiris, Ptah, Su, Seb, Apollo, Set, Thoth, Helios, Perseus, Hercules, Tython, and Keb are but few of the many heroes who are the fiery golden Orb that orders our life cycles here on earth. And we humans have lost the sacred knowledge of the divine body as the manifestation of the sun's ray embodied in the material earth form. When man remembers himself as the divine light, his consciousness in unity with light is no longer ego bound by the illusion of separateness. All men know their destiny, and thus must know themselves. Always remember the sacred cycles of the day (deis -dios), year (yeah-yes or sun), and great year which is the larger calendar of processional time. Within these solar movements are the order of life, death, rebirth, and fertility of man as light consciousness. These help him as to the balance of living. Spiritual experience responds to persons based on how they approach it, their honest intent. The spirit reads them and responds as a tailor to a suit, unique to each person in each moment, but knowing the laws of the solar light is intrinsic to harmony in the consciousness of all. Time is change as everything changes in time.

I will tell of another story of the sun. Jesus is opposed by the setting sun just as Horus is opposed by Set: Horus/Jesus is the morning sun and Set/Sat the evening sun set. These are the natural opposing aspects of solar light personified. This does not mean that Jesus himself was not a walking man of Earth; it means the written story of HIS-Story is of the sun. Knowing the old hidden origin of the name Thomas is of keen value to the sun as well. Byzantine art of Constantinople presents Thomas as the twin brother of the sun Jesus as they celebrate their birthdays on the same winter solstice and so born together in opposition. Tamuz/Thomas is said to be the one who originated the cross, this is the meaning of balance through opposition; this is the crossing of the vertical axis of the solstice and the horizontal axis of the equinox each year.

The letter T is the cross and is so symbolizing division or duality, the dual is the illusion of maya ton the hindus. Peter is Ptah of Egypt and Jupiter of Greece, and Paul is Saul of Tarsus also known as Saturn to the Greeks. In this way (T) Thomas is the same name that became Twain or twin which mean double or split, so as Thomas the twin of Jesus represents duality or illusion or Saturn as Saturn's so larges in gravity always opposes the Sun. Saturn in Greek is called Cronus the ruler of time, *The Lord of the Rings*. He rules time so we in bodies will suffer birth, death and decay. But as we ascend our souls transcend time, the body, and Saturn's power. Souls are eternal and not bound by time. The soul in ignorance, trapped in the illusion of Saturn forgets it's eternal nature and needs to unify heart in mind to see the divine unity in all. Christus the heart/sun chakras through him ascend through higher chakras to solar consciousness. So many locked in fear, time, and conditioning refuse to realize the self; its nature, and its creation. They are the builders in refusal as it is known the stone that the builder refuse will always be the head corner stone. Without self-realization, there is no realization. The puppet master's strings are made of control of the body and mind and offer not illumination because the body and mind can only be guided by the immortal soul that dwells within it. Understand time, step beyond Chronos and *SEE* that any vicarious or future salvation does not exist because the future itself never arrives and does not exist. All second hand salvation is merely hypnotism...all salvation, health, or truth is given to him by himself, in this moment, Now!

As the body is cleaned and looked after with honesty, man begins to get the courage to bare this knowledge of the temple. As man knows he has now the knowledge of good and evil, he now has to choose to be responsible for himself.

No other animal has to carry such a conscious load and in doing so he has to repair his splitting psyche with the vigilance of the heart. This maneuver can take many lifetimes or can take him beyond death itself. Being the temple, he must carry the light within himself as he is courageously aware of his interconnectedness to the infinite light of the cosmos. The body holds the walls of fortification with the mind, but unifies creation with the heart.

Thot and I, as was common, walked. When we did, it was either a trail of banter between us or one of complete silence. The walks in silence were always energetically draining until we stopped to view some peak or ridge and then converse about it. I always knew when we began which kind of walk it would be, somehow with no words I just knew. In these cases I would just walk and listen to my own inner dialogue until he stopped me. Always surprised and outraged by how he stopped the silence, every time he would speak to me from my own inner dialogue. He would pick up my thought as I was thinking or speaking it to myself and then ask me something or point something out. It always shocked me out of my head, then I joltingly would realize how deep in my inner dialogue I was. It was never comfortable and always jarring.

We were walking around gorgeous gigantic pillars in what was known as the valley of monuments to the original peoples of this land. These pillars or buttes were magical and massive; you could build an entire town on the base rubble of one. We would trek over the edges, carving trails up the slopes then back down. We went up them just to get better view points and survey our destination. Every time I got near one of these I got electrically charged with energy and resilience, it was like being shocked so slowly, then instead of frightening pain, I received current power. I loved it. We made it past a few large red, jagged buttes then under the same colored cliff walls with gargantuan overhangs carved out by wind and water erosion. These were cathedrals or sound and beauty.

He stopped under one such overhang; it must have been a thousand feet above us. We walked deeper towards its base and from there looking out it was like being in a cave with a mouth the size of a river delta. We sat with our backs against the upward slope, like being in a hammock, in a perfect recline. Looking up to the day- blue sky and the red rock mountains in the distance, he said, "the body is the temple, you know this now but lessons of the heart teach you the rhythmic charges of keeping the body alive. Death is the great spiritual advisor but the heart is everything, the ultimate unifier, the heart is the heart of it.

Heart essence is the source of all diagnosis. It's the seat of intuition and inspiration in man. It gives peace, joy, and meaning within one's life. There is a power to create lies within it and so many people have disconnected from it and wallow in turmoil chasing one trifle illusion after another. Within in it, lies the imprint of all of one's emotions, the heart remembers. Continual stress kills it and zaps the life force from within. It is nature's key note and man can find this note and sing it, but only with his heart. The brain has no such key note but becomes the aid when harmonized with the heart. True awakening is done through the heart but its intelligence must be hunted and cultivated; it is not born with us like reason is. It reigns over the mental intelligence and will reveal to us everything, for it is the universal intelligence.

If one does not find and sing this keynote, the heart will slowly decay. It is difficult to see in one's life that the mind makes continual mistakes while the heart rarely does. And the Lamas of the buddhic and dualistic schools state that the mind, by stopping its thought, does not attain nirvana, but nirvana is only attained by realizing constant compassion in the heart. While the mind has limited boundaries, the heart is the fountain of the creative force. The mind of the wise man becomes eventually the servant of the heart because the heart leads the path to the nobility of being. The mind can trick and disorganize the emotions of being but with the heart the patterns of emotion become organized and vitalized.

The heart is the builder, seer, and knower of the meaning of life and death. This is why the halls of the Egyptian Osiris used the heart weighed against a feather to find the worthy to pass. He did not weigh the brain or any other organ for they hold and reveal only shortcomings of the temple. The mind will, without the leadership of the heart eventually intellectualized itself into misery and polarity. Only by the mind submitting its service to the universal heart does the polarity within man reveal itself as an illusion and cease. Truth moves in man and through him. It cannot be possessed only witnessed. It is reality itself, just as the cosmos is infinite, so is the truth found of heart. As one traverses these lands, he finds truth in his heart, but only so if he has the burning and sincere intent, sincerity is necessary to find it. Once found it is witnessed, honored, remembered, and learned but it cannot be owned or possessed. He moves inward towards himself, his consciousness shifts and he will find no icon, symbol, or archon that embodies truth because truth being elusive is reality itself, the infinite reality, which cannot be conceived by the mind alone. He eventually finds what he calls his personal truth and momentarily pacified must watch it shatter into dissolution. Because truth is infinite and everywhere, he must go with it. The deeper he goes with it, the fewer his boundaries. If he has the fortitude to sincerely see whatever his boundaries are, wisdom will come to aid and unfold them, if his boundaries either be comforting or insurmountable, they will ensnare him. The deeper he goes, the more he experiences, and the more he experiences the more he expands. The more he expands, the deeper the breaths and rhythms of the heart. All this of the heart, in the body, by the light, is for the highest good; for eternity."

As Thot Spoke these deep words to me, I drifted into some surreal daydream and only when his voice stopped did I awaken to find he was not there next to me. His words were just a moment ago, loud and clear and in my presence but my attention was locked to the inside of my head so when I refocused my attention to my surroundings he was just not there. Still I felt like he was right next to me. I was not frightened, I was completely at ease, I just knew he was around and I had begun to know when he pulled stunts like this that he was not gone forever, he was just somewhere else. I began to know he was like a guide and a friend who seemed to always be there when necessary. I guess by now I trusted him.

I moved toward my bundle of things I had packed and had with me. Inside my backpack was another small bag, I pulled out my journal. It was a little red bound book with black abstract lines resembling tree branches. My dear friend Elizabeth gave it me about fifteen years ago, when she knew

I filled up my previous note book. She must have known it would serve and help me assemble my thoughts. She was and is a very special woman, born on the 20th of march and exhibits a powerful self-motivation and passion in her life. She has a strength, unique and palpable. I opened my notebook and moved through the pages of years of thoughts and notes. I would just write down anything that I felt was or will be important to myself at some time in my life.

I read, then sunk into quotes and words that edified or highlighted what Thot was guiding me through. Thomas H. Burgoyne wrote "death is the grand terminus of one cycle and the commencement of another. Mortality is the harbinger of a still higher state of life, and consequently the forerunner of immortality". Thinking about these words I remembered a time when I felt I was near dying or near enough to seriously contemplate my dissolution. I felt a deep love for my family, my mother and father and two brothers. A sad pain formed in the back of my throat, the kind of pain when holding back tears. This is where the inner smile is formed, that smile you can sense in some people but cannot see it. It's in the chamber of heart and mind connected. It's real, it's the shifting fascia behind the molars and in the upper throat, where you gasp for breath when frightened. This sphenoid area is intimately connected to the sacrum at the base of the spine and affects the subtle energy of all movement of the body. I only know this because I feel it from time to time. When in fright or smiling jubilation within, this emotion or energy in motion moves us, tip to tail.

I read my notes, the words of the Toltec came into focus and tapped me on my retina. Don Juan spoke these words; "The one being warriors can count on and give their entire love to is the mother earth. The one being we spring from and also go back to. She is the spiritual matrix that the loving spark of our being comes from. As a warrior who leaps into the abyss of death, he needs all his wisdom, strength, and forbearance. Just as a warrior who stays here on earth needs the same. Birthing into the next world is just as disconcerting and strange as coming out of your previous mother's womb. It is no easy maneuver and should not be taken lightly. In your world honor it, be impeccable, guard it with your life. Forget the self and you'll never fear anything."

The Toltec path does not seek control of others or profit. It teaches man to go within, to where all truth and reality reside. It acknowledges the body as the temple of God. As the body is natural and produced by nature, its uncorrupted state is harmonious with nature itself. There are great and wise teachers and shamans and masters of the light but no outside saviors; all this is intimately enfolded in the body.

There in the temple of Dendera in Egypt, is the oldest painted zodiac pressed on the ceiling above. Why? Because this is the science of all sciences and was known worldwide in ancient times. The zodiac, tracks the celestial spheres and gave birth to all myths and religious, figures and stories. It is science because encoded in the stories are true and accurate movements of the cosmos, telling us the time, space, and order of the day. Current material science loses this importance; it has forgotten its own origins. The rationalism is so limiting and binding that it has lost sight of the source of its own fractal. It is self-absorbed and stuck in fear. So often science fails to see that humans birthed science. Man is not only the source of technology, he is the original technology. There is no detectable science without the discerning mind of man.

The zodiac at Dendera is more than just a painting; it is symbolic and imbibed with philosophical meaning. The art has within it the artist himself. The floor of the temple is the earth and the ceiling the sky. Columns are the connecting relationship between them. They connect the stars with humanity. The temple is the living art embodiment of cosmic essence and acts as a living book of sacred knowledge the initiate walks through. It speaks to the human through volume, scale, symbol, number, time, and light. It's as above, so below-connecting man to cosmos just as the human body is cosmic connection. Cosmic light enfolded in dense matter. And it be designed and known that at the very center of man is heart, at the heart of it is the heart.

11

Edge of Self

Thot and I talked, really I mostly listened. And in doing so in times shortly thereafter, I began to sink deeper into my meditation practice. I drifted with eyes open while lying down, drifted away. Breathing was effortless and conscious but the body felt as if it was dissolving in the inhale and exhale of my breaths. I sunk into a type of hypnotic lock, where I was seeing with my mind, even though my eyes were open. I went into and through a point on the ceiling, it was tiny and hexagonal. The Point was a stillness of focus. I went to it, right up to it, then through it. Yes this was in my mind, but mind is not simply within my head, it is within all of space. I think I drew into myself the still point but it appears that I went out of myself into the point. Reality is and exists within. As I went through that point I kept going, I stretched thin, cordlike thin across the chasm of consciousness. It was inter-dimensional. I was aware of my body and aware of other dimensions at the same time. I had control of my thinking and was repeating to myself what I was experiencing. I did this so I could consciously remember it when I returned to grounded body consciousness, sense consciousness.

I told myself to get pen and paper as soon as I could move and control my body. I told myself I would remember this experience no matter what, that it was in me and able to be recalled at will. I knew I was functioning on multiple dimensions and could reason with my mind, myself, and my intent from each viewpoint. I was seeing the stars form each of their own vantages simultaneously. It was brilliant and peaceful, it was knowing that I was knowing all in this moment. I even knew that my body knew what was happening. I felt shifts in my nervous system and fascia system as if they are one. I felt pain in head and jaw hinge, and neck but it didn't bother me. I was able to place my attention on higher dimensions and rest there. I had knowledge of how the body, bound by sensation, records and traps pain and painful events inside of itself. I knew I was breathing but sensed an undertone of much longer and deeper breaths spanning over many waves of my normal pace of breathing. In these longer frequencies the moment between breaths was much longer than typical breathing pauses. There was a stillness in between inhales and exhales that lasted. I was not breathing, I was deep and still and in that I was traveling through the light, stretching further and further.

I had a vision very difficult to articulate. It was a straight and diagonal line across my view, a slanted horizon descending from left down to right. The left side was darkened and the right was glowing with light. Dead center, a dark point. Changes in gradual hue of colored light surrounded the dark point, gradually shading closer and closer to the point. Waves of flapping filaments of light hairs became brighter as they stretched away from the point. It was a starting point for light to spiral; the spiral gave birth to the effect of darkness.

I knew I had to write this down, and I knew it doesn't fit into words or language. It was so abstract yet balanced in two things; intent and form. Consciousness is the still point, everything else is its creation. This incredible vast and infinite expanse we perceive and participate in is named reality and resides ever inside the still point. The causal still point shines and moves ever curving in spiral. As the point moves a curving tailpiece of the point unfolds from within, creating the spiral line of light. This in appearance looks to split or divide itself in two but I feel this is an illusion. The darkness follows, or tracks the light line of the curve always a part of but a step behind the light. This is the darkness created by light and gives birth to the effects of cause. They are one and the same but differentiated by degree. The darkness will always track the light and this generates the ground of being we know as equilibrium. This creates the dual arms of spin. All is in motion in the universe except the still point, the center. This is the start of spirit.

I felt this spiral in the body, it started in the back of my head, above the occiput and ran through the sutures of my skull, from the crown chakra curving down behind the hinge of my jaw but just above it, in some small space I cannot describe. I am only aware that it's there I have no words to describe the feeling of it. However, I feel it is the beginning of the creation of my body, the original cell infused with the light of consciousness. This point of singularity, may be the start of the spinal column nervous system.

Darkness tracks and chases light. As light creates itself

from the point of stillness it moves in curves and spirals. Darkness is ever chasing it, and paradoxically manifests all of creation. All creating the dance of light. The spiral starts in the human body from the crown sutures down the back to the hinge of the jaw through the occiput into the point of stillness. This point is the balances that begins the embryo of the human body. The nervous system pours up and out of the sutures of the crown, spills over and down to encapsulate the entire body as fascia. The fascia is a toroidal field and extension of the nerves themselves, causing incredible sensitivity to the being. The still point is over spilling and encapsulating the light of the body and the point of balance. The spiral runs head to feet creating duality in the manifesting body. The entire process is one exhalation, one letting go, one constant movement of release. This is the equilibrium of reality.

Going through the still point of consciousness reveals multi-dimensional stretching out into infinity. The more stretch, the more equilibrium becomes revealed. The entire point of consciousness truly encompasses infinity. It is an inward movement that is God, an inward movement of consciousness that has no end, no boundaries. It is that endless point of consciousness that stretches through the singularity that manifests all vibrations of the spiral. The point of infinity within my own body. I could see that the fractals in the universe always move and unfold through a tiny point, they seem as shapes of random flow but when seen from a large enough vantage they reveal incredible order and pattern. The wave breaking in the river or how the river floods a valley only appears in disorder from a shallow viewpoint. The reality is that the freedom and grace of the movement is unfolding and creating newness in the universe never before occurred. The pattern is still harmoniously ordered by the laws of dimension and nature. The human body is the consciousness of the point at which the fractal carves itself anew into the moment. I saw the colorful blotches birthing from a crack in space/time moving in spiraling curves of lace-like webs of light. The point or creating impetus of this movement was the consciousness of man himself as a co-creator of thought formed reality. I was seeing some higher part of man as unified with the source of light. Light the spitting out of new stars by the Orion nebula, man in his higher form has the potential to break free of the fractal spiral and become a new point of light leaping off the pattern. The greatest of humans can focus their attention so brightly and in tune that they launch off the pattern as freedom and begin a new unfolding of fractal consciousness, still curving as light does but never seen before this current moment of time. A star is born.

When you reach the still point within, which is consciousness itself, the body falls away and reality in its oneness reveals itself. This awareness is what is called soul, the individualized piece of spirit or light. If we suppose that the infinite all/omnipotent consciousness is truly light itself, then we see that all its manifestations are enfolded into ranges of density and that all matter is and must be in motion. The omnipotent infinite is still and causal but all else is forever in movement at some level. So planetary bodies are not only created from light they are powered and guided by it, meaning that without light they stop spinning, rotating, and orbiting, and even stop being. Our human body is thus the same, bodies powered, ordered, and created by light. The body is the temple of divine light geometrically and mathematically enfolded.

Let it be known the true origin of man is divine light,

and once you, the seeker on the path of knowledge, gain this realization, it is your duty to care for this knowledge and keep the temple clean. Recapitulate your thoughts and emotional interactions regularly. Sit with them and discharge your emotional entanglements with others and yourself. This Toltec practice is very valuable and freeing and results in harvesting energy to shift to higher attention. Process your darkness and do so, not in fear for you're the lamp that shines light on your own darkness. And take not the pity or blame others of sinister minds who throw their darkness upon you, for you are the lamp and where the lighted lamp shines darkness cannot abide, this is law. People clean, their bodies, beds, bushes yet spare not a moment to clean their emotions or their psyche. The sinister have systematically killed our great masters, shamans, and medicine people in the attempt to kill their ancient wisdom too. But to no avail because, the sun rises in Aries upon the vernal equinox of the galactic plane now in the northern hemisphere, and the lights angles that beam from there are brilliant and ushering in a higher age. We take heed to clean our consciousness and sharply question the teachers of institutions today, it is pointless to be led by the blind. Reality is of a spirit nature and material things only effects. See the unity in consciousness and of religious paths. While the cult of Aton destroyed the library in Alexandria Egypt to stop unity consciousness from spreading, the sun's great rays reveal now the depths of the edge of self.

Seeing the fringes of the self, as it is formed through light, causes a paradox for me. As I study and piece together a conception of the self, in this case the experiencer, I began to always come back to the same conclusion. It is a conundrum, or in brighter terms a zen koan. In these meditative and mystical states, deeper levels of self are revealed and I feel progress, insight, and clarity but then realized that I (divine ego) am still always the witness, the observer of these deeper states. So I can't seem to dissolve the ego, or when I do as soon as I realize that I realized something, there the ego pops into the field claiming the new insight. As this happens over and over, I began to shift my belief about what is the ego and why does Burgoyne call it divine? I began to see that paranoid conditioning over my life has always been cautious and fearful of this ego and taught it was maleficent. Once seen with the eye of unity, the ego is divine. It is the boundary or resistance in every moment beckoning me to unify and transcend. It's divine nature is so intrinsic it is the body or form of the harmony of consciousness itself. Meaning, the divine ego is present as the wave in the ocean, they are one and the same in essence but the wave would have no pattern, body, or form if the ocean were non-existent. The divine ego, is not created to be devilish, it is there to pattern the growth of evolving consciousness itself. I began to see I didn't need to fight the ego, I simply need to love it because without the presence of the illusion, there will be no point of reference to detect the real.

The divine ego is spirit infinite in personality, and germinate in man immortality. The soul must learn to remember it's immortality within the infinite consciousness to awaken. This is what awakened or enlightened really means. The soul must compassionately care for the divine ego and then harmony can birth the note of the infinite. The divine ego is unbound in its potential but still ordered somehow by the infinite god. The divine ego is only limited by its own dissolution; the I is limited by itself. Here, another cyclical paradox and still the divine ego designs the soul and only limited by its own design and expresses the cosmic consciousness through the soul. I knew that higher consciousness revolves around conception (sex), the unifying of all that is to continually be birthed into awareness. The act of conception literally creates life in manifested form. The trick, then, is to embody this awareness so as to never forget it again, even traversing through the great door of death. This is total freedom.

I told myself to never forget. Never forget that reality is what is actually real (now). I repeated it, reality is what is actually real, not my limited perceptions of it. It's so simple. The ultimate split of gender, which generate, created the self; male and female joining together in union to create. The action of sex is such a strong compulsion for us not because of its intense pleasure but for the deliberate placement of the self into the stillness of the present moment. It brings us in direct awareness with still point of reality; what is real, the fabric of existence.

So, in this awareness, I exercise the renewing of mind every day, it's not necessary to renew experience each day, but mind is the element needing to be renewed, as it tempers the nature of experience. I feel I am now addressing my emotional immaturity and maybe the culture at large too. We have developed our physical prowess, so as that there is no ocean or mountain we can't chart and categorize. We have developed the intellect using technology supreme still this is a failure until man develops his emotion or energy in motion to reach his full maturity. This is what I see happening now in my current and modern time; the emotional aptitude is the barometer for superior vantage and quotient. This is symbolized by the long term orbit of Pluto and Uranus, as their unique light reflected by the sun will remain and influence life consciousness here for up to 200 years. Man must transcend his childlike fearful emotion and claim adulthood and maturity. He must balance himself according to the solar harmonic. It is time for the ant to recognize the elephant, so to speak! Man is a multi-dimensional being, physical, emotional, psychic, and spiritual. Looking into our emotional current state, we may see that the birth/creation of the ego may be due to ancestral and or catastrophic trauma, and if so it is not the self (a reflection of light or cosmic consciousness), because self is always whole. This is to say that the ego is a split or fragment due to trauma, then inherited to children through generation and so is conditioned to only respond or react to further trauma. It is not creative as a fragment for only light (being whole) can create. The darkness can only subvert or twist what is already created, darkness has no ability to create, it can only plagiarize, subvert, or steal.

The emotional state is thus displayed by the values and moral code of man toward the Mother Nature. When in his fallen state he displays disharmony with nature and is violent towards her, when enlightened he is in care and a keeper of his center, or to say he moves from his center of being, He knows thyself! In unification of self, or wholeness he stands under the eye of immortality and is unified in oneness, he is tuned to the nature's harmonic. He is, in this state real. He is pure energy and in his highest state expression he s nature's indefinable. He is pure awareness not bound by time and tapped into cosmic potential as he dissolves his body into infinite consciousness.

Just how does this occur, the dissolving of the body? The human DNA offers the mathematical and scientific answer. DNA employ Phi ratio of 1 to 1.618 to embed perfect nesting of energy as waves within waves to magnetized toroidal fields of consciousness causing perfect sharing, also called bliss. Perfect sharing is bliss as it is an energetic loop of self-perpetuation and growth with no loss of energy. Plants display this Phi ratio as leaves branch higher and higher without blocking their own absorption of sunlight, thus sharing with the self and causing bliss within the plant being. As this self-sharing/bliss is recognized within the being, it is stretched and promoted as it is harmonically attuned the all-natural cycles and the cosmos. Each Phi ratio displayed is a wave nested within a wave from shortwave to infinitely long wave, once harmonized rings the spell of love. When man in the body does this by way of thoughts, mentality, emotionality, and spirit his blood becomes electrically charged and ascends to higher vibrations which in turn express recursive nesting of deeper waves nesting in a loop of bliss.

This is also known as perfect embedding or fractality. Long waves converge with short ones in harmony. In the human heart it is called emotional coherence. The intentions of the pure heart are emotions of share-ability and rise to higher and higher level of consciousness. Over time, sorting through the emotions we come to thought, emotions of pure principle and there is no hiding in us, as we know we're of pure heart and intention. The heart generates its electric field of pure share-ability or bliss and others feel this as well. In pure share-ability or bliss, you go through implosion or kundalini, so deep inward you expand the field of awareness and being toward the infinite field. The Greeks called this the elysian fields of consciousness. You can recursively repeat this implosion into ever deeper fields. Man has always looked to the few spiritual giants we call sun gods to do this for us and heed their wisdom of such a maneuver, it being wisest to realize each man can to this for himself. He may transcend separateness, through perfect sharing and become the Holy Grail, the cup with no inside or outside, but the void in the spine of the DNA itself, the dodecahedron formed in man, Earth, and zodiac alike. It has been stated that mind sleeps in the plant, dreams in the animal, and awakens in man.

I am remembering the initiations of the old Hibernians. How I recall these is unknown, it appears in me as images of old memory. My soul is imprinted by image, experience impressed into me. These impressions shift my perception so as I may never forget the specific kind of knowledge it has led me to. It is a knowledge ever deeper of intimacy of the spiritual world. By striving to know self, carefully the self is impressed with being and is initiated into higher knowledge. The maneuver is the initiation into being and out of material consciousness. This is becoming aware of our intimate death consciousness, also known as awareness of our constant annihilation. The body dies continually. By disintegration we become aware of the potential to experience the spiritual consciousness we call being.

The experience of deep metaphysical states combined with time in contemplation and stillness in meditation was beginning to mark progressive shifts in my life. My everyday routines and works were more cerebral and conscious. If I kept aware of my breathing throughout the day, I could function in the present moment while simultaneously being my own observer. This was stress relieving and reality revealing. I began to deepen my knowing of myself by peering into it from a higher, more sophisticated vantage. The edge of self. This was easy at first but after a few weeks, the boredom of routine and less time in meditation, it began to give way to comfort of routine. The state didn't leave my memory, it simply became harder to replicate.

Still these states prompted my approach to self-discovery to be uniquely different. I, with a creative side, can understand numbers and symbols with more depth and syntax. I used the study of ancient symbols to discover their many layers of meaning. Symbols are the key to attaining abstract reality, which is absolutely necessary to transcend the intellect. Transcending the intellect is a must for wholeness or universal mind knowing. If one does not exercise or engage their abstract creative mind, they are crippled with a crutch and cannot link or sync themselves to all that is.

Symbolism is the language of dimension and the voice of nature; she is volume, form, light, and color. And those who don't see this, are the crippled and don't see that their own personification of these natural symbols are the very ignorance and antipathy to nature. All of man's higher expression is transmitted to him directly from nature (neter) and cannot be resonated by his physical senses; he must use his more subtle sensitivities, those of the timeless architects and artists. He cannot rely on reduction and reason to reason himself into wholeness because wholeness lies outside of the intellect and outside of reason.

The feminine aspect, herself the mother, will stand and watch while the intellect imprisons himself into material illusion while he longs for her intuitive nurturing breast. I had a flashback of a conversation I once had with Thot, just outside the cave from which I emerged. I am unsure as to when exactly this time was, but I remember the subject we spoke about. Immortality. He had brought this topic up before, mostly in reference to the ancient Egyptians, referring to their culture viewpoint as the meaning of life.

They strongly believed immortality was a perfected state of consciousness and attainable.

He said, "the ego is divine. It has pure positively if you give it the freedom to be so. Or it can have pure negativity if you give it so, with your divine will. The negative view of the ego is what most people are taught to believe in; they are taught fear. If you identify with fear, then of course your ego, your divine ego will be fragmented, scared, broken, and unaware of its true nature. So drawing on some great minds; Pythagoras, Heidegger, Alan Watts, Kierkegaard, Blavatsky, Jung and many others talk about the unconscious. We hear them saying, that if you procure your divine ego to gain an understanding of immortality instead of mortality, its divine nature begins to come out in you.

The bible clearly communicates in 1 Corinthians 6:19, "you are the temple of god for the temple of god is holy which temple you are". Deeply and clearly in most ancient texts of mysticism it state the same, in order to come to this realization one must *know thy self.* Gospel of Thomas "when you know yourselves then you will be known, and you will know that you are the sons of the living father. But if you do not know yourselves then you are in poverty and you are poverty." Here we must not look out at the dysfunction of society to cast blame, for if we do so we do not know ourselves. Change occurs in conscious intent to know who we truly are and no one can impart this reality upon us as reality is co-created each new moment. It unfolds and appears as the path beneath our steps just before we place our foot down. The path reflects and rises to meet us moment by moment.

Getting at the self indeed is elusive as it is not connected to any type of learning we have been taught, it's a remembering. The way to get at it is apophatic in process, which means it's not something you gain, attain, or control, the self won't allow such a meager approach. Through apophatic knowledge you have to uncover everything that is not the self to then see what is self. Until we know what is false, what is true remains hidden from us. This is a maneuver of letting go, not one of attaining. It becomes a sharpened skill or training, and ability to discover what is not, leaving glistening in the light, what is. Most importantly this maneuver when learned becomes the creation of self itself. Meaning, we don't find the self under the rubble of this deconstruction, we create it in each moment letting go of what is not reality. Through this ongoing experience the self is created, as you. And this why no one can impart selfhood upon another. No pope nor guru can give it to you; at best, if truthful, they may be able to share their own experience with you. Tricking yourself into believing otherwise is the mechanism of disempowerment, social masks, and self-avoidance. The power of being is the still point of center. If you were to see yourself as a mathematical representation, as many of the ancient mystics do, you will find yourself as the I or number one. The one, but with a reducible nature. Pause and open the abstract part or edge of yourself, and hear. The one in which you, in material form are reducible, because your body exists in form. You are divinely created from *the one* that is the irreducible one; which being the source of all, has no form and no body. The irreducible one cannot be reduced or divided, because it has no body to be split or divided. The irreducible one is active in principle so masculine and electric, it then decided to manifest form. In so doing this act, replicates itself by splitting into two, now duality is born. In the number two now exists both active and now passive principles, so now both masculine and feminine. In the number two we now have duality, so the irreducible gives birth to duality and duality is really just equilibrium as all manifestations exhibit a dual nature. All of nature manifested is dualistic or the state of equilibrium.

Out of the number two, (which now exists) arises three principles. The third principle is born of procreation, so out of equilibrium, a new process is made, procreation (the created, is now co-creating). And the third principle is power, which gives rise to the geometry of the triangle (3 angles) in perfect balance and harmony. Three equal sides, three equal points, pointing upward is how the irreducible one manifests all that is (quality, quantity, principle, idea). The irreducible one builds a trinity and man in material body is dualistic in nature, we are both mortal body and immortal soul. Man is nature's equilibrium enfolded with spiritual power.

When you see that part of yourself you become aware of your own immortality, your own divine nature. I believe this is our human true design by spirit. And many people think that immortality doesn't exist but by using simple example of striking a match, we may see the contrary. The wooden match is the body and the flame is the life within. We strike it to see the flame appear and dissolve through time the body. The life light appears to stop and go away, yet we strike another match and a million more to see the light flame appear always. The same flame arrives and is never diminished. It is powered by the ground of being, divinity, or God.

Here on Earth that power is given to us through the planet itself, by the combination of elements, oxygen, nitrogen and so forth, allows fire to always be here. Opposers would say, out in space flaming potential is not there, but it is actually there. It is just in a different form. The ground of being is still there, as light. It is the light of the sun that powers earth and creates its own unique signature of light that also powers the people. And of course our solar system is powered by even larger star systems and then galaxies and by the universal ground of being itself, the infinite! The point is to wrap your mind around and identify with the immortal part of yourself, the nagual.

The mystics all speak in their own voice of this type of experience. Mystics, like the great seers, and naguals are pegged and identified by such experiences, without them, they are just ordinary people, confused and afraid by the descriptions of realities of their society. Intently seeking absolute truth, the mystic becomes the mystic. I see that it is not through the intellect one can arrive at such a place because the function of the intellect is to break up the flow of consciousness into small segments in order to categorize and describe reality. It, the intellect, has no means of detecting or experiencing the infinite. I move beyond the mechanics of the intellect into the boundless and once there center myself to the deep awareness of the abyss, the unknown, the imaginatrix; where all dead souls pass into transformational processes. This is where all destiny lies and all futures and pasts dissolve. Coming into the center of being. Man is not created to peer into reality but to be embedded within it, where the center, self-directing, communes with infinite consciousness. This maneuver is accomplished only by individual personality, uniquely balancing truth/reality with individual super conscious potentiality to see creativity finger tipping the life force of source creation.

Since man is a conglomerate of luminous reality

clusters, he often distracts and confuses himself through multiplicity. He will mystically see by seeking the absolute that he will never find satisfaction by placing his center within his intellect, for it is a box of names and walls. He will not bathe in happiness intellectually living in the descriptions of the world or of himself. Deeper into inner space he must go to pierce the lattice of the mystic and be spiritually alive. He feels the light of moving away from the world of the senses and deepening his awareness of the divine and active, infinite consciousness. It is a deeper state of union, as unity is vitality to ascending consciousness. With his bodily temple he is dual, both being and becoming simultaneously, still, he is not fragmented. He holds his center balanced mystically on the edge of both points, not dividing himself but unifying it. Only the real can know reality! Reality to him is two-fold. Power is beckoning us through struggle, by creation power splits and opposes itself (us) forcing us to unify the middle path. Through infinite division it creates a paradox of opposites which reflect itself in new moments and new ways to shine infinite viewpoints. This is the pattern of the cyclical sacred hoop enfolding and unfolding. As light is undetectable without its contrast of darkness, resistance and metaphysical synthesis percolates.

Pounding the harmonies of the drum or string, music is brilliantly created through intuition not intellect. As man is bound by the paradox of creation, his mortal body intuitively sown into eternal spirit is singing his highest potential consciousness as beauty in harmonious resonance with the sound-song of creation. He is the muse, he is music, he is mystical.

The mystic learns how to move between the worlds of the living and the dead, not because the dead are morbid but because the dead are asleep in a consciousness of self-slavery. The mystic, sees, smells, and magnetizes the keys to the absolute, opening any gates that keep him mesmerized in the worlds of phenomena. As he moves through the ranges of worlds he must share his heart, his artist souls with others, to willfully inspire them to commit to their own sovereignty and creation of self. The mystic is secretly in love with the infinite and most of those around him have no understanding as to why. But he alone, has access to the transcendent reality and the creativity charged within it.

He is sacrificed by struggle as noted prior. The mystic is identified by being in some sort of struggle or pain; be it physical, emotional or psychic. This pain tempers his spirit towards intuitively listening to the transcendental beat of creation and offers the forging of perfected temperament. He must heed the primal call of divinity laced in creation and when he does so, power collides with his self, disintegrating the ego of self-importance. This is the entrainment of the central self to transcendental reality, satori. He is now able to be his own lamp of light, he is deeply rooted in the central created self but desirelessness is still to be achieved. It is said that to attain the state of desirelessness, the will has to dissolve personality completely. It must be a state of surrender, although I do not know for sure. The mystics say their lives are from this moment on, in a perpetual state of ecstasy. The reality of the sense world has no relevance anymore and living is now super conscious and intensely vital.

Looking in from the edge, we see the common cosmic creation story all having the personification of the christus shaman guide. He in his form speaks of love and in so teaches the NATURAL way to bring the solar temple down to earth. Father sky so faithfully married to mother earth. Old kingdoms in their original footings taught and held this sacred way. Egypt, Scandinavia, China, India, Mayan, Toltec, Peruvian, Druidic, Hopi, and others were among the first after the diluvian floods to work with the angelic angles of light to keep this light for their generations. I see when digging deep into them, their truth.

To bring the temple into material form is man's highest pursuit; it encodes the ladders of ascension and the opportunity of immortality. Immortality, not a vain avoidance or fear of death, but the grand pursuit of infinite potential; the most worthy quest when fearful ego is left out of the equation. Oh levity, be still and feel the rumbling of enlightenment. He learns of the spheres, the seven planets, seven chakras (chi of Ra), angels, or seals. He initiates himself into the mysteries and learns how to harmonize them. These seven realities correspond and connect him to the self, the truth divine and are thus the only dao (way) to unity. And let us know that in unity is the only arcing path to infinity. The great pure spirit, total freedom. All is in the wave, and this merging of short wave frequency with the longest or infinite cosmic wave frequency is the attunement or merging with the ground of being. This vibration we call God, aum, om, amen, atum, infinite. When expressing such a vibration he displays the form of spirals within spirals recursively expanding. Creating fields within fields eternally channeling divine consciousness, peering into itself from just over the edge within.

12

The Red Road

The ways of the aboriginal Amerindians has always been a source of attraction to me. As a young child I felt a familiarity when I would see an Indian either in person or in a photograph. I feel that I could look at them and understand the way they see the spirit world. I may be naive but this is how I have felt since I was a boy. As I learn and grow I began to study their ways and, in their own words and language, I tapped into the deeper message I hear. The communal way of life, the nomadic patterns of the seasons, hunting, and sustaining a life balanced in nature is just natural to me. Even though I didn't grow up with these direct teachings, my time spent in nature opened me up to the vibration of the Earth and her sacred heartbeat.

Into manhood I began to seek out and study a deeper understanding of the Lakota way of life. As I did, I managed to drum up the opportunity to participate in some of the Lakota ceremonies and through this I have learned some basics as to the way they connect themselves to the spiritual realms, how they meditate and illuminate themselves. I don't claim to be well versed in such things or have a depth like that of someone who grew up in the culture but I still evolve deeper and deeper each time I participate in ceremony and their sacred prayers. I also see the connection to many other paths and philosophies through them. Much of my learning has been from a medicine man named Lee Plentywolf on the Pine Ridge reservation in South Dakota. He has taken the time and patience to share with myself and others the beauty of his line of medicine. Lee is a holy person whose heart and mind are working in tandem and his keen awareness of those around him is the mark of a true leader. His humble approach and his words hold power to heal and shift the consciousness of others. The shaman has the ability to move the assemblage point of reality so as to see a new paradigm and defragment the deeper mind that may be hold you back from wholeness.

I witnessed proud strength of heart, mind, and character with him and his family at the annual Sundance ceremony. Some things these people do will open your heart and eyes to things you would not consider possible for humans. The level of connection and commitment to spirit and the eagle's emanations is brilliant to witness and be part of. In short it is sacred! Not all that is written here comes directly from Lee's teachings, some I have learned along the way or from others but his soul vibration is, I believe in line with these words.

"From the North, where the giant lives-

to where you always face (the South)-

the red road goes, the road of good-

and on it shall your nation walk!

The black road goes from where the thunder

beings live (the west), to where the sun continually

shines (the east), a fearful road a road to troubles

and war" (Black Elk).

The red road is a circle of people standing hand in hand, people in this world, people between people in the spirit world. Star people, animal people, stone people, river people, tree people...the sacred hoop. To walk the red road is to know your ancestors, to call to them for assistance. To walk the red road you have God given rights. You have the right to pray, dance, think, protect, know mother, dream, vision, teach, learn, feel happiness, fix wrongs, truth, and the right to the spirit world. To walk the red road is to know sacrifice, suffering...to know you will one day cross to the spirit world and you will not be afraid.

My time with Lee Plentywolf is special. I remember preparing a sweat lodge with him and some others. On March 23 just after the spring solstice (although in almost all ancient accounts, March is primus (latin for first), so really the first month of the zodiacal year and the sun's ecliptic).

My great soul sister Elizabeth Upton invites me to attend the lodge. Elizabeth has been a woman of spiritual magnitude and a loving friend to me since she was just a teen girl. I remember the sacred moment when she was adopted into the Plentywolf family. She is the one responsible for bringing Lee into my life, I thank her continually. So as we prepare the fire and heat up the grandfather stones, we make prayer ties imbibed with the heart's intentions for healing and growth and love for all sacred beings. It's takes most of the day to build a sweat lodge and nothing is rushed. Your actions are conscious and meditative to prepare your body for the intensity of being re-born from the womb of the earth.

Lee instructs us on when and how to prepare ourselves for the purification ahead. He exhibits a holy vibration, it's palpable, something I can feel in my body. Others feel it too. He leads the prayer in the sacred way of his people and graciously shares it with us. He knows it's sacred and there is no question; his vibration helps and heals those around him. He vibrates in such a way his ancestors and good spirits listen to him as he calls to them. Just before entering, as we pray, a large red tailed hawk comes to the yard. He perches just a few feet away on the top of an umbrella table. He is on that pole, listening and watching us. Most birds would have no part in the affairs of humans but this hawk is resonating a blessing with us. He stayed there for at least five minutes, looking with his regal obsidian eyes directly at us. You can say this is just happenstance but the more I am around Lee, the more these type of things happen. Hawks are solitary hunters and avoid people and groups of people but this one came in our group to make his presence known to say aho mitakuye oyasin (we are all related)!

Another lodge, a similar event took place, and at the same time, just before we entered the lodge. Lee was praying and calling in the allies and ancestors and then he began to purify each of with the sage smudging. The sweet and delicious smoke cleans your energy field and thoughts. He was near me and spoke softly, he said look up there, way up high, straight above us. At first glance I saw nothing, they were so high. Then I saw them, circling, there were three eagles straight above our heads, I mean as if they were attached to us somehow. They were definitely very large birds and I could tell by the shape and wing span. My thought was, how could they be eagles, how does he know. As if he read my thinking he said, they could only be eagles; no other birds will fly that high. I know condors may, but in our location there are no condors. They must have been eagles, looking our way and making their presence known.

These eagles feel and are in tune with his heart, they sense his calling. He has this mystical way about him. "You turn into whatever you tune into". The eagles bless our ceremony with their far reaching vision; they bring us the clarity from their high and luminous vantage. And they hear the call of the natural ways of the Lakota and Lee Plentywolf.

A year later I was invited to a function in the cause of rescuing and saving the wild horses of the southwest. A wonderful woman invited me; she is in her own right quite the horse whisperer (if I may use the term). Beautiful Jane Wesson and I went to the function together and there we met with lots of interesting people and gathered and learned and donated and ate in the company of like-minded souls. Towards the end of this evening, a Navajo/Comanche healer asked to chat with us. We jived immediately and his kind heart shone through his movements and body language. We shared stories and I let him know I have practiced ceremony of his ways and people and connect in such ways. He offered to smudge us and bless us with prayer and sage smoke. Of course I said I would be delighted. Jane and I followed him into the back yard and he prepared himself and we did the same. His eagle feathers fanned the sweet smoke burning our way. He covered our aura and energy with the smoke from head to toe, all the while gently chanting and speaking his native language. Our eyes closed and going within, my intent going inward to peace and reception. I could feel Jane doing the same. Our hands connected us in this blessing, it was beautiful!

His name is Daniel Ramos, he was deeply involved in our evolution at the moment. He began to speak in English (quietly), it was intimate. The things he said to Jane were intense and packed with knowledge and direction. I tried to follow but it was too much to remember. He spent much more time with her. He knew her heart was open and special, he knew she was spiritualized. When he moved to me, he said "I am a keeper of the fire, it's my journey and my nature to keep watch of the fire. The fire is what burns in our heart, our authentic self, our desire as a spirit. The heart path is one closer to spirit and our real self." He also said our spirit heart (not our eating heart) is on our backs and that mine needs to be sealed, and that "in this time I am shifting now to seal my spirit heart; to a path, to the red road. Aho!"

This was a powerful thing to hear and feel from someone I just met, but I knew he was in truth and I felt at ease receiving his wisdom. She and I went home in good vibrations, while remarking at the remarkable evening. I took time to digest his simple message. He meant that I walk with a wide open heart, he saw it in me. The Grandfather spirit spoke through him to help close my spirit heart. If left too far open, the chaos of many spirits can attempt to influence and sway me, distract me. They're not necessarily bad but I need to be aware. Grandfather was looking after me. I have become friends with Daniel since this, and he and I were attending the Sundance together but at different locations. He will always be in my respect and kindness. Enlightenment is realizing how much you don't know! These types of encounters spur me on to connect, to know how much is beyond, the Great Spirit. We turn into what we tune into.

Invigorated, which is unusual upon my waking state, I moved out of slumber across my tiny yellow kingdom to manifest a stellar cup of coffee. As I sat and sipped, I began to wonder what is the conscious waking reality? And what is the sleep and what is the reality we call life, and then what is death? Intuitively I sensed in myself the understanding that all complex concepts can somehow also be reduced to exquisite simplicity. My experience with practicing Native American ceremony brings me directly to this precipice. I see myself as researching, searching, and absorbing knowledge then being compelled to remember it through my documenting it. But with Native American people, they seem to hold it within and document it with practice and ceremony. I felt the average western man has lost this sacred tradition in his culture due to the dominant value becoming the commodity, or finding a way to monetize everything, even the sacred. This is not the way of the red road.

Insight and memory pooled in my thoughts of the medicine wheel, the sacred cross encircled. In astrology and many ancient cultures this symbol is the symbol of the earth.

The Dogon, Druids, Chinese, Hindus and others use this symbol as Earth because it is the knowledge of agriculture man, he used the sun and planets to chart and calendar the seasons for growing. The serpent or sun shines light that hits the rotating earth at angles that cause it to undulate up and down in sine wave patterns along the equator. The crest and trough mark a vertical line while the equator marks a horizontal. The intersect of the light wave patterns on the earth is the hielo (holy) cross.

Agricultural man used the sun to keep sacred cycles for all of life's meanings and ceremonies. They drew a circle on the ground with a diameter twice the length of a chosen post or stick, then stood the stick upright in the center of the circle. Marked the points on the circle with the longest and shortest shadow occurred in a year. Drew straight lines from these points across the circle and where they intersect became this symbol, not only of the four directions but of the yearly solstices and equinoxes. The two days during the year when the shadow falls directly in line with the stick and these points mark the equal days. These days are sacred, as nature designed our solar system; nature designed this expression in the 24-hour day and 365-day year. It is the natural time keeper. The serpent sine wave also keeps time in the human body as this light wave runs through us regulating out power, pulse, yearly rhythm and life cycle. Why have we forgotten this? Because man has as many masters as he has vices. Monetizing the sacred is a detrimental vice.

Man can easily lose his way and he will know he has done so when he looks for his own face in nature and finds she has not reflected it back to him. He being short sighted by his possessive and fragmented ego fearfully spins out of control when he sees not his reflection in the sacred around him. His visage is so fragmented and blurred it does not register to his own mind' he has nothing sacred within himself. The more frightened he becomes the more self-destructive he gets. Old peoples of the Middle East so proudly brutalized their neighbors then erected structures and statues then worshiped them as images of themselves, slowly forgetting about their own creator source. Unjust and proud, they were told not to build a sign on every high place for personal amusement or to build fine buildings for yourselves with the hopes of living there forever. Those peoples were told and warned if they did so, they would be seceded for such attitudes. Babylon fell, tower and all.

We are interconnected to everything at our subtle levels and collective conscious is supported by the earth herself. When people are in tune with nature, this is so apparent and knowing this we see our collective levels. Once you see deeper into man, you see beyond the illusion of our separate bodies and find our energies eventually merge in finer and finer filaments of light in deeper dimensions of one universal source. The bridge to the spirit world is real and we are all relations.

The sacred is the red road, and it's a perceived reality as real as any other, once you learn how to see it. The Amerindian or Toltec view of perception...strength rests in the clear assessment and refinement of yourself, permitting you to launch yourself into the unknown. The following are words of Ken Eaglefeather, an apprentice of the known Toltec seer Don Juan Matus, the great Yaqui nagual. "You learn to relinquish yourself to a universe that is quite beyond human awareness, but which is completely incorporated. The quest is to live fully the essence of your life, the path of continual self-discovery. As for the Toltec a distinct advantage of this view is that, regardless of philosophical or spiritual orientation - such as whether or not one regards themselves as having a soul - grounds the experience in the here and now, in this life, in this world." This concept doesn't negate God or spirituality. Rather, it can be used to enhance spiritual awareness. Instead of defining our experiences by our occupation, location, or nationality, for example, the "human being comes first", offers a stable, concrete reference point for all to connect with. There are eight cornerstones of Toltec perception; reason, feeling, talking, dreaming, will, seeing, tonal view, and nagual view. With that awareness we can utilize different spiritual orientations to increase everyone's quality of life...

The Red Road, is a unique perception of the Native Americans and the Central Americans and South Americans, the Toltec is one of the best and most organized ways to tap into the Red Road. "It comes from a predilection that puts the human being first, this means that we must first know ourselves not just our personalities but our true design and makeup in nature. When we start from the human first perception we are able to keep things honest and true more often" -Eaglefeather.

The Red Road is a road of sacred and honest spiritual practice regardless of culture. "The Toltec, he is dreaming, he shares from which other dreams emanate. Making it possible to handle the immensity of infant perception, it furnishes a reference from which to explore. This generates spiritual evolution. In its entirety, the Toltec Way is but one path weaving through infinity. Like Buddhism, Sufism, Daoism, and a host of other systems, it requires that, to follow it in earnest you must make it your principal path.

This does not mean that you can't participate with other philosophies. It means that you must fully traverse its course in order to know it, and then be able to leave it. To use its boost of spiritual power, you must practice it. One of the most appealing things about the Toltec way is that it requires its practitioners to take things further, deeper, wider. The Toltec way simply will not rest within the status quo. It is a constant path of self-discovery." -Ken Eaglefeather.

Understanding that the human being is so dynamic, typically needs a system, a system of thought or approach to their relationship to reality. The system can be thought of like having handrails while walking down stairs or up a ladder. Most people need the handrails, but only until they find their true center, and their balance that is inherent within them once they cultivate the awareness of that balance. Toltecs work to integrate thought, emotions, and behavior, leading to a complete integrity of personal energies. This like many systems becomes a way of living and not so much a religious bind. "For all good and ill, a system determines what is perceived, understood, and realized. On the downside, instead of being used as a tool for learning, it is molded into what eventually becomes perceived as the ultimate reality. The person then remains lost within it. On the high side, it engenders a personal transformation in which the expression of personality reflects behind and beyond personality. Behavior emanates from an intimate connection with all creation rather than from social conventions of ordinary or non-ordinary realities." - Eaglefeather.

The idea here is that human beings are a bundle of awareness; we are designed as energetic intelligent awareness at our core. Desire and intent become powerful forces within our reality and personality. It is important to see that our inner world upholds a great deal of the character of the outer world. The inner world, where the intent and logos (or word) is born is where total freedom exists. It's just that so few are aware of this and those who uncover it rarely engage in the exploration of its creative power. Desire and intent can both distract from and add to reality just as light and darkness can prompt our awareness to expand or contract. These forces are much more fluid than people think and this scares all but a few very peculiar people, those indomitable people are caller warriors on the path of knowledge.

Eaglefeather explains, "The energy body connects directly with the world. It offers a sense of knowing our natural place in the universe. But as our evolution has thus far developed, we now interact with the world through another field of energy that principally uses symbols - rather than direct communication - to the structure of reality. We develop this field through our thoughts and familiar feelings about our world. Hence this field generates a reflection of reality. The conditions of reality we place into it echo back to us." So here he is basically confirming Jungian, psychology, that the nature of the unconscious is specular and it reflects back to us the massage or face that we shine into it.

Eaglefeather often engages the idea of intent as existing beyond desire. The spiritual intent, superseding our physical wants and assumptions, becomes the energy that we perceive. In that way, "Manifesting your core nature leads to being, a state of balance and harmony with the world" - Eaglefeather.

"Intent consists of focused or condensed energy. It embraces the essence of a person, place, or thing. It exists beyond desire. It is quiet certainty. It is the energy of alignment, the energy required to shift the focal point. Thus is the energy that controls what we perceive. Proficiency in shifting energy and moving the focal point determines what you manifest, or what you bring into conscious awareness. Manifesting your core nature leads to being, a state of balance and harmony with the world. Throughout all of this is power, which I also defined as divine will, or spirit governing our steps. Power supersedes all forms of personal power because all forms of personal power flow from power. So everything has its own power. Through expanding awareness, personal power increases." Eaglefeather...There's something to be said here, about systems or guidelines for perceiving direct knowledge of reality or truth. Every culture sets up a system that determines how people think and perceive reality.

As the more sensitive people in their culture become shamans, the shamans hold and teach the way, which is sacred. But it should be known that these ways sometimes evolve and devolve. One of the beautiful things about the Toltec, is that they acknowledge this relationship to power and reality itself, and allow it to be as it is, free flowing, and unfolding before each person as they walk each step of their path. "Technique and method should always rest subordinate to a personal relationship with power. So when they lose their power of keeping you with spirit, it is best to just let them dissolve and go about your business of living. Then let them dissolve into growth, however, not from lack of effort. The work is always your - the individual's - responsibility. And it's not simply that you realize an understanding, but you realize you're being."-Eaglefeather

Consider an alternative viewpoint, or perception, you

don't have to believe it or put faith behind it, just consider it as a new vantage point or a new jumping-off point into reality. Consider that the self, is not something you're born with. Consider that the self is something that you create while you're here throughout your life; you use your thoughts, creativity, memory, and experiences to put it together, and mold your own reflection and call it the self. If this is true, one can never find themselves, because the knowledge of the self, is not something you find, it's something you create. In this process of creation, we use a specific type of knowledge and a specific type of learning that is typically not taught in schools. This type of knowledge is called apophatic knowledge, which means that one must discover everything that the self is not, and what is left or revealed is truth, and the self. Through apophatic knowledge, or the stripping away of everything that is false, truth is all that remains. The idea of soul, is a religious syntax, and refers to the psychological version that which may be called the self.

If the self is created in your own experience throughout your life, then you see a huge shift in power, as you realize, that no one can give you soul or self. No priest or hero or authority, can bestow the self upon you or funnel it into you, this makes you responsible for creating and caring for the highest version that you can conceive of yourself. This takes you into the process of the red road, or the process of being your own sovereign shaman. This is the divine right of all human beings, as we are designed with energetic awareness at our core. So at some point, you have to let go of the handrails and be centered in balance, and move beyond all systems that secretly teach you that you are limited, or separate from the infinite consciousness. The systems that acknowledge, that you are infinite consciousness, are always transcendental in nature, and pointing a path towards total freedom, where you yourself become to be as you are truly designed in nature, harmony.

Gospel of Thomas- *when you know yourselves, then you will be known but if you do not know yourselves, then you are in poverty, and you are poverty.*

Learning about the self, is as I said before, not attained through typical means of learning. You cannot get at it by stress, strive, attaining, or gaining, or grasping. You can only get at it by stripping away the falsities of reality, by stripping away everything that is not the self. The self will be that which remains. This is why this process is always unfolding before each step that you take along your path, and also why no one can give you this knowledge; they can only share the experience that they had while uncovering themselves and hopefully motivate others to walk the unfolding path themselves. This process, is a bit abstract, but once engaged in, you become comfortable in the balance of seeing the path unfold before your feet as you pronate on it, at first this is a bit scary, but the better you get at it the more brilliant it becomes, and the more in the present moment you are able to live, and tap into, and create the self.

The point is, we must engage in this process, and walk along the red road, and understand that it is much more fluid and much less rigid than we have been taught. If reality, is our mirror, and everything is interconnected which it is, this means our approach to reality, our jumping off point, will be reflected back to us. And the more universal and unifying our approach to reality, the more brilliant our self shines. The unconscious is spectacular in nature, which means it is a mirror. The path to total freedom will reveal itself within the self, as you approach the path with the freedom to be who you truly are. Separateness, is an illusion and some want to hold that power over you by secretly teaching you that you are separated from the cosmos, the infinite. But if reality is specular in nature, and you shine separation into it, fragmentation will be reflected back to you. If your greatest heroes and gods are heathens and rule through fear, then the limited self that you create will be just that, constantly in fear. If you reflect hostility and fear into the infinite unconscious, then you will meet demonstrative beings along your unfolding path, just the same, if you reflect or approach the unconscious with courage, sovereignty, unity, love, and heart, you will meet the most brilliant of luminous beings. By deep voyages into our own inner space, we can heal. We heal when we see trauma (mostly ancestral), causes fragmentation of consciousness which by reflection appears as the pseudo self. The persona/mask it wears if not cared for will perpetuate the trauma as antipathy to nature, our own nature and the natural world around us. The fearful grasping outside the self for social approval begins and is reinforced so much that a neurotic dependency develops, which if not curtailed fosters shame, guilt, and self-hate to such a degree disowning the self becomes an option, but only so as a grand illusion. In this state love and spirit seem to disappear.

In the depths, no matter how dark, we find center. In special times in my life I have been invited and showed up for meetings with power. Power, flowing through us is always beckoning us. I met Lee Plentywolf and his family and many others for my second Sundance ceremony in Manderson, South Dakota. During this four day ceremony people give themselves to spirit, to heal the planet and bring forth medicines for the heart of earth peoples. Describing the ceremony itself is pointless, my words would fall short. It's something that can only be experienced in the moment.

I will offer up some of the symbology to present some meaning for the perceptive heart.

The four directions of the circle, is a sacred circle, the sacred hoop, the cycle of life, and the four directions are the four cardinal points of north, south, east, and west. East is yellow, west is black, north is white, and south is red and there is a story of a bear living in the hills of Crazy Horse at white horse creek. One old man built a sweat lodge to pray in and asked the Great Spirit for a sign, for guidance. He was told by a medicine man to build a mole hill in the lodge with fresh mole dirt, and in this action a symbol will appear for him. So he did. He waited at night and in the morning there was a paw, a bear paw imprinted in the mole hill. A bear came in and delivered a symbolic message for him. And that bear represents the bear magic, the bear power, the strength of the bear to pull us through hard times and to teach us to temper our spirit. That bear represents a star constellation where the Lakota people came here from, which are the (to the best of my knowledge), the pole stars of the earth's axis to magnetic north. They believe their ancestors have gone back to those stars and that they travel from the spirit world back to Earth from those portals and stars and through the light of the sun. As above, so below; they come from above as spirits and when enfolded below they take on flesh bodies and form.

And that is how we traveled here and how we get back. We travel a spirit road back to the sun and stars of the sacred bear. And so they dance; they do a yearly Sundance for the sun and cycles of life on earth. And the sun in a year, gives us the four seasons, which are the four directions. Because the sun travels in spirals and the earth orbits it, we get the harmony of the four winds. The tree placed in the middle of the sacred circle represents the tree of life and the sun powers the life/tree and we pray to tree to keep that cycle of life going.

When man came here from the stars his energy was infused with the Mother Earth so the earth would continually give birth to him and support him. He was first just a liquid, a blood. He had no body. As the blood percolated from the earth, the buffalo, the great buffalo nation tasted the blood and really liked it. They drank all the blood and man could not come through long enough form a body. They were happy but as time went on, they grew curious to see what would happen if they let the blood run out and live. The buffalo nation became curious because the plant nation spoke to them. The plant nation made a pact with them and said let the blood flow out and let the people be born. If you do this, we the plant nation will feed you always. We will feed you the grasses, the plants, and herbs we will be medicine for you.

So they agreed, and so man came out of that blood and formed clay and that clay formed a body. Man was born of the womb of the Earth. And that is why the buffalo made a pact with the plant nation and the plant nation and the buffalo nation both made a pact with man. And man so made a pact with the buffalo nation to take care of all the four-legged creatures and to honor their sacred spirit. To keep the sacred hoop of life going, they honored the pact that the buffalo had with the plant nation and they all honored each other and vowed to keep the cycle and sacred hoop going forever. This is why we Sundance, why we pray in this way, to honor the sacred cycles of the great earth and the great sun, and the Great Spirit. Aho mitakuye oyasin (we are all related).

Insight comes from within, this is why it's called IN-sight! In some eastern esoteric traditions, it is shown that the Buddha/Buddhist thought does not concern itself with the nature of God, it is concerned with the nature of reality, which is always now. This may be why Buddhism has no creation myth or story. Where we come from is beside the point, because he (Buddha) has uncovered the ground of being, which is always here. By feeding the body nutrient it is healthy. By feeding the mind its proper medicine which is meditation, settling in the current moment of equanimity, reality is revealed. Through practice of being in the current reality it became obvious that to transcend the suffering of the body, the divine mind must be implored. In order to move beyond the divinity of mind, we must awaken into the highest consciousness. Here we see thought does not exist, it dissolves and all that remains is the infinite.

The mystic is different from the ordinary man because he consistently engages in the process of seeing absolutes which is to say he walks the red road. He is driven from deep within to be unsatisfied with the stories of other men's telling of truth. He must experience it for himself and make up his own mind. He is his own. This is the same man in the west called a man of knowledge or a warrior on the path of knowledge. If he practices, he may align himself with power which will at a specific moment offer him the personal power of learning to *see*. For him, reality is not absolute being, it is absolute becoming. The constant and dynamic flux of creativity. He is committed and engaged with absolute and self-evident knowledge which came to him through pure awareness. Always in his life and story this pure awareness is tempered and afforded to him by way of religiosity, suffering, and beauty; which are the universal teachers of the absolute. "The eagle does not demand our reverence to it, it only demands we fill ourselves with awareness."-Castaneda

The mystic connection with the absolute is not bound by culture, time or space. With this connection they see reality directly as it is, time and space do not tamper with the experience so they are creativity, each moment. He realizes that our description of the world is ultimately a work of art not a work of science, because our senses we use to build science are born originally of our creative nature. Many cling to science as the ultimate because it claims to have uncovered universal constants and people need constants to feel secure. But Science becomes honest with itself; we see many of those constants are actually much more fluid than we first thought. There are many examples of this and they tend to rattle the rational mind. One example is the rotation of our Earth was said to be factually spinning at an exact rate for thousands of years until during each processional cycle, it slowed down briefly when in proximity to the star known as Sirius. It eventually sped back up but see the rate was changed by the gravity of another star. We also see that gravity bends and affects light so what science so rigidly seeks to prove is constant is really proving that the real dependable constants are systems of freedom, fluidity, and ever new change. We create our sense based science and it is an exquisite mystical art. He knows and upholds his universe by knowing himself.

When I sink into myself and touch moments beyond time, I touch eternity. You may laugh or scoff, but in vain as it is true I do such things. And you and others do them also. It is but a state of awareness that is knowing thyself. Denying this awareness is just blurred vision, or lack of seeing or clouded attempts at being. I sat awake, vitally awake by being and when doing so, it is so stark and apparent the difference between wakefulness and sleep, between the cave and the cosmos. Still, so surreal and obtuse is it, when I know I am asleep again. Like a light, like a candle I am turned off then on, lit then extinguished, brilliant then absent. Thot, sat with me again, outside a cobbled stone path that lead from tall pines to a cavernous sea side. We spoke in pleasantries, and smoked our pipes; the smell of sage and cedar embraced me like a grandmother from before my time in the womb. He asked if I knew anything at all that was certain? It took me a moment to speak but I knew emphatically the answer was yes. I replied, I am my own, and no other. He chuckled and puffed his pipe, relaxed were his eyes.

He said "here on earth, we learn, it is so important we learn who we are and how best we learn." He went on. "One thing we need to remember and then digest is that when we think about the ancients, their writings, and what they meant, we almost always come from our current mechanized viewpoint, which is highly material and highly intellectual. We must realize that when the ancients looked in nature and described it and said they saw luminous bodies around rocks, trees, and animals we must realize that they actually saw this. We here in this time often write this off as fantasy but when we dig deep into our own psyche and our own soul we realize that the ancients were perceiving reality in a different way. They were able to perceive nature as closer to the soul and further away from the intellect that we do today.

I have spoken of this before; the ancients were more holistic in their approach because they were intimate with their own annihilation. It's very abstract but you can follow this thinking. Man seeks to destroy or annihilate himself in some strange and absurd way. With technologies we create or even insights that come to us through imagination, we see that it is in his nature to at least think about destroying himself. This is why we have a shadow side. Being a sentient being he seeks to annihilate himself not in a sinister way, but for the greater good of all. As paradoxical and absurd as this sounds, it is no different than viewing a fractal in motion. The fractal is constantly evolving, dissolving, and curving its edges into a perfect pattern of rhythmic harmony. Much like a solar wind effectively prunes the branches of the cosmos. With man's psyche he seeks his own annihilation not to destroy himself but to remind himself of the immanence and pertinence of being. Can you follow this? Can you follow this logic? When we are faced with our own destruction, for example the great equalization of death, we awaken to the pertinence of life. It is in the awareness of our own destruction, we forever renew ourselves. We forever open our minds and hearts in consciousness to the expansive infinite. This knowledge of our own annihilation is what keeps us moving ever forward into eternity. It strangely keeps us aware and constantly evolving our souls.

The wars of men are reflections of this chasm of change. The more aware a person is of his true nature in infinite spirit, the less he wars with himself and others. The dark forces are shattered persons who cannot create, nor procreate light. They have only the small ability to distort light already created by immortal beings. The dark forces attempt to sell you any clever distortion they think you will buy. They do so, so you will forget how to procreate the light of consciousness for yourself and depend on them as an outsider to define who you are. If you buy their distortion, they control the imprints you accept in your soul. They decide your wants, purpose, personality and desires. This is the meaning of the phrase the devil will steal your soul. Each soul is a constantly evolving creation governed by the self in which it resides and if you allow others to create it for you, then your sovereignty and immortality will not be realized.

It is the masterful awareness of self-realization that must be awakened to perceive truth and reality. The creative design is that God must experience these thoughts while in the physical manifestation in order to realize them in eternity. In order for them to be made an active principle in the spiritual world is to perpetuate higher and higher awareness of self immortal. This evolving self-reflection is the fundamental reason for creation at all. Man's physical body is the role of consciously evolving spirit. Only certain thoughts can be thought when in the physical body and these must be carried through the gate of death before they can be made active eternal principles in the spirit. And so it goes, the one verse, the great song, the universe actively creates its immortal self." Thot, smiled and said, "It's about each one of us creating and shaping our unique and individual cosmology. No one can do this for you."

I could see both him and myself in perfect clarity. I felt grounded and at peace. The soul and consciousness being specular reflect our approach to it, and today our approach is so hardened, rigid. The result is current generations only teach ourselves to be further and further away from our spirit. The auras that exist in nature are always there, though subtle, the human soul and higher perception is always available to them if we just realize our deeper connection to them, then like a secret they will be found. Now, I will speak about why the ancients were able to see these auras much more readily than we today. It has to do with sleep; their sleep was more intense and more rewarding than ours today. This is because of their daily tasks. They didn't use or build a mechanistic world. They were not strengthening their reality with the intellect, or have a linear perception of time, or reward the clock at the end of the day. They were much more harmonic with nature, and were able to see deeper into it, as well as their own souls.

Sleep is a polarity to wakefulness just as light is too dark, and hot is too cold. However, in our current society, we don't prepare our soul or our mind before we sleep. We don't recapitulate the emotions of the day; we don't take care of our souls like the ancients did. In sleep, the dreaming world is a reality beyond the physical body. The waking world, the tonal, is the consciousness of the body while the sleeping world is the consciousness beyond the body. Both polarities have power and reality. It is our society that has lost these teachings, and also erroneously rejected them. Only this rejection causes our own suffering in our soul. One must realize that sleep is incredibly important, the sleep or dreaming world is connected to our consciousness outside the body and brings forth changes in our consciousness that is waking inside the body. The ancients used to prepare themselves for sleep much like a meditation or prayer; they would dive deep into this world and give thanks for the blessings of divinity in which they lived during the day. This dreaming world would spill over into the waking world each day and their reverence for the higher worlds, higher powers, higher consciousness, and of course their own higher self were much more present in their lives. In simple terms, modern people would meet the ancients, and be astonished by their brilliance and keen insight into themselves and nature. Modern man would simply say; *that person has soul!*

It is paramount to understand how the ancients related to their own sleep in order to understand the ancients themselves. Modern man, often looks at the ancients as being obscure, thus we lack understanding because we do not understand their self-work. The ancients used to sleep as a way to work on themselves. It is only in sleep that man can truly work on himself, in the dreaming body, dreaming world; the world outside of waking consciousness. In essence, they had a beingness in the dream world, they were sacred there. Modern men, have lost this sacredness in their sleep/dream world and so it is reflected in the polarity of his waking world. He is losing his sovereign and sacred awareness. He is losing himself, while building mechanistic structures in his head and desperately praying that they will save him from his own destruction.

Consider that he may educate himself into forgetting his own *will to force*. It is important to see that the education of the Ancients although we may think more fantastical than that of today, imparted more rewarding knowledge for the culture of all of humanity as a worldwide whole. We may not realize that even with our highest technologies and our keenest intellect of today, we are regressing instead of progressing. There have been cultures in the past that far superseded our current state of consciousness, we owe great respect and awe to their accomplishments even though we are unaware of them. They did things in nature and art with more soul awareness. Even sleep was an act of prayerful communion or soul. They had contact with the divine forces in a way much deeper than us today. It is what the human being of today secretly longs for, the human of today longs to know what it truly is to be a human being. Only in his soul, his individual soul can he know. We look to the ancients, because they knew something we don't; for example, the sacred use and meaning of words.

The writing and words of this book, are not meant to be headspace, and intellectualized. In ancient times the reading of a book was to invoke the intent and inspiration of the will of the reader. These subtle energies were drawn out by the reader whenever a book was read or spoken, the intent of the book was not to be intellectualized it was to be realized with the soul of the being. Stop and think about this, Think about it with your entire body, your energetic temple, your being. Don't just use your head; think about these words with your heart.

I understood him completely. He said, remember the druids and their initiations. The druids spoke of science as knowledge that lacks being. And art is fantasy that lacks truth. It is only in the being of man can he discover meaning in these, only he that dwell in the eternal. He must first learn how to transcend the body in order to be present, only then is the power granted to him to see behind the veil into deeper reality. Man can, by employing his will and intent, unite the polar opposites of subjective realities. He becomes one with them both and gives meaning to his life and creative soul. Through his own logos the power of his word is born in reality as crystalline/Christ consciousness. Initiation is the cultivation of experiencing the consciousness between death and rebirth.

In a peaceful walk to the torrential sea, we went to watch the energetic arc of the rising sun and in stillness before the breeze begins all was right with me, all was right with the world. I only had a zealous feeling of gratitude. As I stared long at the sun, I could sense myself standing upon it, as if a part of my awareness was there. Causal still light is infinite and its manifestations are but self-set into motion. It is the dreaming. Awakening is still. I follow a wave, watching it crashing on the craggy shore, watching it rolling through me, then I awake. So peaceful, was my awareness of lying in a bed of bliss. I asked myself a question that I, moments ago, just answered. The Gods being so divine, where did they decide to hide wisdom so it will be out of the reach of man? The one place he will never look for it, within himself. I lay there keenly aware of my wakefulness. I did not get up. I stayed there, well rested, in a state of suspended animation, and silent. A rumble, a resonate tone thrilled through me as if Gabriel's trumpet pounding through the drum of my chest. I heard the words I AM, and large wafting wings around me and a light within.

Dedicated to the human spirit-

"The world floating in a sea of the infinite and resting in night shows the present state of humanity. But, the blush of dawn is ready to gladden the soul, and the expectant seer, from his lonely vigil on the hilltop, awaits the sunlight which will soon flood the world anew".

---Thomas H. Burgoyne

Made in the USA
Columbia, SC
25 August 2018